IT ACTUALLY HAPPENED

TRUE STORIES OF THE WORLD'S BEST SWINDLERS

DUPED!

ANDREAS SCHROEDER

ILLUSTRATIONS BY RÉMY SIMARD

annick press
toronto + new york + vancouver

This book is the first in the It Actually Happened series.
(text) © 2011 Andreas Schroeder
(artwork) © 2011 Rémy Simard

ANNICK PRESS LTD.

Edited by Catherine Marjoribanks
Proofread by Laura Edlund
Cover design by theBookDesigners
Interior design by Daniel Choi Design & Communications, Timothy King
Cover and interior illustrations by Rémy Simard
Telegram image (p 139) © istockphoto.com / Jill Battaglia
Forged bank note image (p 109) courtesy of Lee Richards, www.psywar.org

We acknowledge the support of the Canada Council for the Arts, the Ontario Arts Council, and the Government of Canada through the Canada Book Fund (CBF) for our publishing activities.

ONTARIO ARTS COUNCIL
CONSEIL DES ARTS DE L'ONTARIO

CATALOGING IN PUBLICATION
Schroeder, Andreas, 1946-
    Duped! : true stories of the world's best swindlers / by Andreas Schroeder ; illustrated by Rémy Simard.

(It actually happened)
Includes bibliographical references and index.

ISBN 978-1-55451-351-2 (bound).—ISBN 978-1-55451-350-5 (pbk.).

    1. Swindlers and swindling—Juvenile literature. 2. Fraud—Juvenile literature. 3. Hoaxes—Juvenile literature. I. Simard, Rémy II. Title. III. Series: It actually happened series

HV6691.S334 201   j364.16'3   C2011-902078-5

Printed and bound in Canada

Published in the USA by Annick Press (U.S.) Ltd.	Distributed in Canada by Firefly Books Ltd. 66 Leek Crescent P.O. Box 1338 Richmond Hill, ON L4B 1H1	Distributed in the U.S.A by Firefly Books (U.S.) Inc. P.O. Box 1338 Ellicott Station Buffalo, NY 14205

Visit our website at www.annickpress.com
Visit Andreas Schroeder at www.apschroeder.com
Visit Rémy Simard at www.remysimard.com

CONTENTS

2   INTRODUCTION: TOO GOOD TO BE TRUE?

6   THE TASADAY: STONE AGE CAVE-DWELLERS OF THE PHILIPPINES

22   THE GREAT SHAKESPEARE FORGERY

40   WAR OF THE WORLDS: A MARTIAN INVASION

56   THE PRINCE OF HUMBUG

70   INSTANT GLOBE CIRCLING—JUST ADD WATER

90   OPERATION BERNHARD

114   LA GRANDE THÉRÈSE STEPS OUT

132   GOOD VIBRATIONS

150   FURTHER READING

151   BIBLIOGRAPHY

154   INDEX

157   ABOUT THE AUTHOR AND ILLUSTRATOR

INTRODUCTION
TOO GOOD TO BE TRUE?

In 1916, an American named Louis Enricht announced that he'd invented a cheap additive that turned tap water into automotive fuel. While World War I raged in Europe and gasoline sold for a whopping 30 cents a gallon, Enricht claimed that his additive would bring the per-gallon cost down to a single penny.

They did—and it worked! Enricht's demonstrations were so convincing, in fact, that the world-famous automaker Henry Ford offered him millions for the rights to his additive.

SOON, YOU'LL BE ABLE TO TEST THIS IN YOUR OWN VEHICLES!

Actually, Enricht had merely discovered that if you add a very cheap chemical called acetone to water, it will run an engine—for a while. Then it will destroy it. But before anyone found that out, he convinced not only Henry Ford but several other famous American businessmen to give him millions for his worthless invention.

When we hear about a scam, we might think: "How could those people have let themselves be fooled so easily?" It would make sense if only stupid people fell for scams—but intelligent people do too.

So what makes perfectly smart people fall for crooks like Louis Enricht? Sometimes it's just greed. It's one of the oldest motivators of humankind, for both the scam artists and their dupes.

Oscar Hartzell, a failed farmer and rancher from Iowa, understood that well when, in 1913, he contacted everyone in the United States whose surname was Drake. He told them that, due to a bureaucratic bungle, the estate of the famous British pirate Sir Francis Drake had never been paid out to his heirs. It had been gathering interest for over 300 years and was now worth 4 trillion dollars—enough to buy all of England, Scotland, Ireland, and Wales! Hartzell invited Drakes from all over North America to invest in his campaign to take the British government to court to retrieve that money. He promised that everyone would make at least 500 dollars for every dollar invested.

Most scam artists fool their victims into giving them money. Some, however, are after love or power or fame.

You wouldn't believe how many people fell for that scam. Tens of thousands! Hartzell was able to move to England and live like a king in a mansion. The FBI investigated his story and announced it to be a lie (Sir Francis Drake's wife had received her husband's estate in 1597), but people kept sending Hartzell their money.

Well, some might say, that was a long time ago, people weren't as sophisticated then. But consider some of the scams that operate today, like the famous "Nigerian Letter" people have been receiving via e-mail for years. In it, a close relative of a Nigerian politician informs the recipient that the politician managed to smuggle a fortune out of the country before his recent death. If the individual agrees to help, the relative will give the e-mail contact 25 percent of the fortune.

Then the scam begins. The person being scammed is told that a "security company" will pass on the fortune when they receive an administrative fee of $2,000. But it doesn't stop there—more requests follow: a customs fee, a notarization fee, a clearance fee, and so on, as long as they can keep stringing someone along. At no point does the person targeted receive any payment. Thousands of people get duped by this kind of scam every year.

Greed drives many scams. But so do need and desperation.

Hartzell was finally arrested, tried, and sent to prison. However, the flow of money didn't stop until he died, in a prison hospital, after operating his scam for over 30 years.

The people who fall for these scams do so because they want this solution to be real. They're willing to invest their hope and their money in the tiny possibility that they might really get what's promised.

An urgent need, or the desire to reverse bad luck, drives many stories in this collection. A young Englishman resorts to an extraordinary scheme to win his father's approval. A yacht race contestant with a leaky boat finds success in an ingenious way. A French peasant cooks up a clever ruse to win the acceptance of high society.

Not all scams are amusing, but the best of them are totally fascinating. The following 8 stories explore some of the most inventive and outrageous scams of all time.

THE TASADAY
STONE AGE CAVE-DWELLERS OF THE PHILIPPINES

This scam not only made headlines around the world, but also duped world-renowned scientists into rethinking their theories about human evolution.

THE PLAYERS

The politician, the tribe, and the world that watched them

In August 1971, a helicopter with four passengers and two flight crew took off from Davao Airport on Mindanao Island in the southern Philippines, headed for an unknown destination. Only powerful government officials were allowed to keep their flight plans so secret. The helicopter was under the command of Manuel Elizalde Jr., head of the Filipino Ministry for National Minorities and a close friend of the president of the Philippines, Ferdinand Marcos.

A month earlier, the Filipino government had made a stunning announcement: one of its agents had stumbled across a small, primitive tribe hidden deep in the Mindanao jungle.

Known as the Tasaday (taw-SAW-day), these seven men, six women, and fourteen children were still living in caves as their ancestors had done thousands of years ago. They had never encountered modern society and still used only stone and bamboo tools. They wore loincloths made of leaves or grass and ate only foods they could gather—wild fruit, yams, tadpoles or frogs, palm pith, and worms.

The news caused an uproar throughout the world.

For anthropologists and paleontologists, this was like traveling back to the Stone Age without using a time machine.

The Filipino government was swamped with requests to meet, interview, photograph, and study the Tasaday—not only from scientists, but also from newspaper and television journalists. Some of them threw clothes into bags and grabbed the next available flight to Davao Airport, hoping to hire local guides to take them to the Tasaday.

Elizalde had made it clear that he wasn't about to have the Tasaday overrun by anybody. Those who wanted the privilege of studying them had to file a proper petition, and then get in line and wait. Only those studies that had scientific value or might otherwise yield some knowledge of importance to humanity would be considered.

Anthropologists and paleontologists are scientists who try to unlock the secrets of how our ancestors lived and evolved. Without ancestors to talk to, they have to piece history together by examining little bits of bone and fossils to imagine how ancient people and animals looked and lived.

MOST JOURNALISTS HAD NO IDEA WHAT AWAITED THEM. THE TASADAY CAVES WERE HIDDEN IN A MOSTLY UNMAPPED PART OF SOUTHWESTERN MINDANAO.

IF THEY MADE IT THROUGH THE JUNGLE, THEY'D FACE THE ARMY OF NATIVE WARRIORS ELIZALDE HAD HIRED TO KEEP PEOPLE FROM REACHING THE TASADAY.

WITH ELIZALDE AS THEIR CHAPERONE, THE JOURNALISTS FROM THE *NATIONAL GEOGRAPHIC* HAD NOTHING TO FEAR.

Elizalde was the son of a rich and influential Filipino family, and he had not shown much interest in native issues or, for that matter, selfless causes. He was very smart and could be charming, but he was also aggressive, rude, and careless. He liked money, spent it recklessly, and was known as a party animal. A lot of people felt he'd been given his government appointment because of his many political friends.

At the same time, he'd surprised people. Even though his family owned large mining and logging companies in the Philippines, he'd come out strongly against the invasion by such companies into areas inhabited not just by the Tasaday, but by native tribes all over the Philippines. Within days of announcing the discovery of the Tasaday, Elizalde established a Tasaday Preservation Fund that immediately began accepting donations. Even though Elizalde had said access to the Tasaday would be granted based on the scientific value of the proposed studies, if an applicant's donation was big enough, concerns about scientific value were swept aside.

Meanwhile, rich television networks like America's NBC and Germany's NDR, and newspaper and magazine publishers like the *New York Times* and *National Geographic* quickly moved to the front of the line.

When Elizalde launched his Tasaday Preservation Fund, many prominent groups joined him to help raise money. President Marcos was applauded around the world when he announced a year later that he was setting aside a 19,000-hectare (47,000-acre) section of the Tasaday jungle as a protected native reserve.

THE ENCOUNTER

The Tasaday meet modern humanity

Back in the helicopter, the passengers saw the jungle stretching like a solid green carpet in every direction. An hour after take off the pilot began checking his instruments more often. A few minutes later he put the aircraft into a steep dive. Soon they were hovering directly above the dense jungle. That's when the journalists realized how they were going to "land."

A WHITE-KNUCKLE DESCENT DOWN A SWINGING ROPE LADDER BROUGHT THEM TO THE FOREST FLOOR.

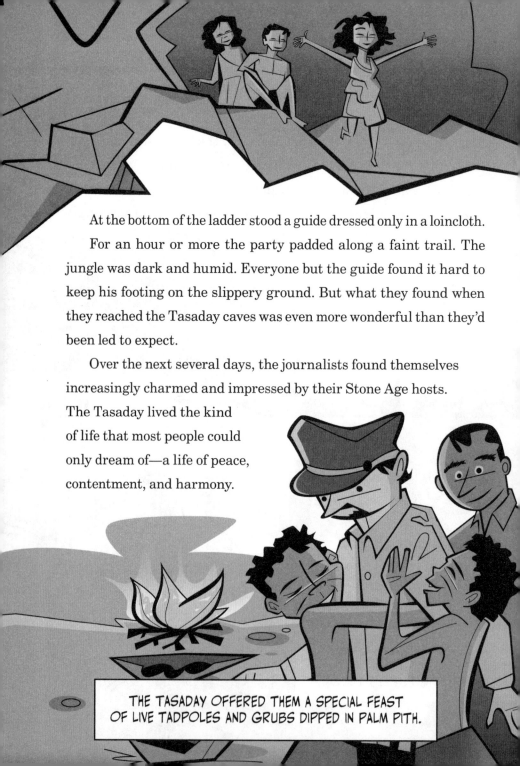

At the bottom of the ladder stood a guide dressed only in a loincloth.

For an hour or more the party padded along a faint trail. The jungle was dark and humid. Everyone but the guide found it hard to keep his footing on the slippery ground. But what they found when they reached the Tasaday caves was even more wonderful than they'd been led to expect.

Over the next several days, the journalists found themselves increasingly charmed and impressed by their Stone Age hosts. The Tasaday lived the kind of life that most people could only dream of—a life of peace, contentment, and harmony.

THE TASADAY OFFERED THEM A SPECIAL FEAST OF LIVE TADPOLES AND GRUBS DIPPED IN PALM PITH.

THE LOST
TRIBES
OF THE
MINDANAO

NATIONAL GEOGRAPHIC RUSHED ITS
FIRST PHOTO ARTICLE ABOUT THE
TASADAY INTO PRINT, AND NBC BROADCAST
A FOLLOW-UP DOCUMENTARY.

FIRST GLIMPSE
OF THE STONE
AGE TRIBE

The Tasaday didn't have words for "weapons," "enemies," or "war."
Everybody seemed to get along. Men and women lived as equals—they
didn't even seem to have a leader.

People the world over fell in love with the Tasaday. The documen-
tary proved to be one of *National Geographic's* all-time greatest hits.
One of its editors enthused, "If our ancient ancestors were like the
Tasaday, we come from far better stock than *I thought*."

Anthropologists were fascinated (and also puzzled) to discover that, unlike most primitive peoples, the Tasaday didn't create cave paintings or make musical instruments. Although there was plenty of raw material available, they had no plates or cups, and they boiled water in hollowed-out bamboo sticks.

They didn't brew alcoholic drinks, and they didn't smoke or chew tobacco. This was really unusual. Anthropologists had never encountered a people who didn't practice at least one of those habits. As well, the Tasaday didn't seem to have any religious traditions.

They did believe that if they stayed patiently in their forest, a Good Person would come to them, bringing much joy and good fortune. That person, the Tasaday had decided, was Manuel Elizalde Jr. whom they called "Momo Bong" (Divine Being), and this gave his visits special meaning. It also explained why they didn't seem to want to have any direct contact with outsiders, even after they'd become aware that other native tribes lived close by. In any dealings with non-Tasadays, they always chose Elizalde as their spokesperson and go-between.

The Tasaday married, but didn't perform big celebrations. When people died, they were simply buried in shallow, unmarked graves without ceremony. When asked if they believed in an afterlife, a heaven, or a hell, the Tasaday looked confused. The questions didn't make any sense to them.

As the stories and reports multiplied, so did calls for greater protection against the advancing logging and mining companies.

RETHINKING THE STONE AGE

Scientists revise their theories

For the next three years, a steady stream of journalists and scientists visited the Tasaday. Now, though, they were allowed to stay for only a few hours at a time and had to be accompanied by Elizalde. Then, in 1974, Elizalde abruptly canceled all further access to the tribe. He said he was afraid they might accidentally catch modern diseases like smallpox, tuberculosis, or polio. He also claimed that the Tasaday were finding the interviews too exhausting, and that their lives were becoming distorted by too much contact with modern people.

However, a virtual "Tasaday industry" had developed and was flourishing in schools and universities all over the world. In 1975, the first full-length Tasaday book appeared, entitled *The Gentle Tasaday: A Stone Age People in the Philippine Rain Forest*, written by the American journalist John Nance. Other books, and hundreds of reports and scientific papers, followed.

ELIZALDE BECAME A POPULAR SPEAKER ON THE ACADEMIC LECTURE CIRCUIT. EVEN THE WORLD-FAMOUS SMITHSONIAN INSTITUTION INVITED HIM TO WASHINGTON TO SPEAK ABOUT THE TASADAY.

THE RENEGADES
Skeptics voice their doubts

During all this time, a few renegade journalists and academics had refused to go along with the excitement.

These dissenters—many of them people who had been refused access to the Tasaday—simply didn't trust Elizalde or any project he was associated with. They felt he was using the Tasaday to get a lot of media attention for himself.

A Filipino linguist suggested that the Tasaday language was too similar to the dialects of the region's other tribes to have remained isolated for thousands of years. He even claimed he'd overheard two Tasaday men in private conversation using words that sounded oddly like "cement," "house roof," and "pickup truck"!

By the early 1980s the location of the Tasaday was no longer a secret. Still, Elizalde's army continued to defend their territory from unauthorized entry. But when Marcos's regime began to crumble, it wasn't long before Elizalde's army—which had been paid by the Filipino government—began to dissolve too.

And why, people wondered, had Elizalde kept all the interviews with the Tasaday so short? Why had he monitored them so carefully, and even tried to control what scientists wrote about the Tasaday?

Elizalde dismissed all these objections as sour grapes. They were simply the complaints of grumblers who were jealous of his and the Tasaday's worldwide popularity. The world's love affair with the Tasaday continued.

THE SCAM UNVEILED
The true origins of the Tasaday

A Swiss journalist named Oswald Iten was one of the first to hear about Elizalde's failing army, in early 1986. Known as a radical, Iten loved to tangle with governments and their institutions. Sensing a scoop, he caught a flight to Davao airport, where he linked up with a local journalist named Joey Lozano, who knew how to get to the Tasaday caves.

The two men fought their way through the rainforest to the edge of the Mindanaoan jungle—becoming the first people to manage an unauthorized entry into the Tasaday reserve. When they arrived at the caves, however, they were startled by what they found. The caves were empty. The Tasaday had disappeared.

This was a puzzle. The Tasaday were not known to travel far. The two men looked around, then began investigating in earnest.

They discovered that, although the Tasaday had supposedly lived in these caves since the Stone Age, they had left little evidence behind. No old or broken tools lying around. No garbage. No forgotten or abandoned personal possessions.

Then Iten and Lozano discovered a trail, camouflaged near the caves but well defined farther along. It led toward the village of Blit at the jungle's edge.

Iten's biggest discovery came several days later when the two reporters finally found the last piece of the puzzle.

They found many of the alleged Stone-Agers living in huts just inside the jungle. They were wearing Harley-Davidson T-shirts, Nike sneakers, and Levi's jeans.

They were also wearing watches and smoking cigarettes.

The Tasaday, it turned out, were nothing more than local natives who had been convinced by Elizalde to pose as prehistoric cave-dwellers.

Oswald Iten hurried home and gave the scoop to a Swiss newspaper. On April 12, 1986, the story was headlined *"Steinzeitschwindel!"* *("Stone Age Scam!")* and ran over three pages. Two days later, the Reuters news agency picked up the story and sent it around the world. British and American television crews quickly followed Iten's trail. They confirmed the whole bizarre story.

Manuel Elizalde Jr., it appeared, had cooked up the Tasaday scam to fatten the bank accounts of his Ministry for National Minorities. As the first millions poured in, he used some of the money to benefit the natives under his care.

However, once Ferdinand Marcos's government began to fall and Elizalde realized he would probably be exposed, he abandoned his promises. In late 1983, he helped himself to the money in his ministry's bank accounts and the Tasaday Preservation Fund—estimated at $150 to $250 million.

THE AFTERMATH

Most of the large newspaper and television corporations that had been fooled were too embarrassed to give the story much coverage. Smaller competitors, however, were happy to give the story attention, and to point out how badly the large media outlets had been scammed.

Those scientists whose reputations were most at risk generally worked hardest at damage control. They gave talks or published papers defending their earlier claims about the Tasaday.

Manuel Elizalde Jr. was never brought to justice—but maybe justice found him anyway. After living the high life in Costa Rica for about 10 years, he reportedly became addicted to crack cocaine and ended up squandering his fortune. He died penniless in 1997—even poorer than the "Tasaday" natives he had used so effectively to con the world.

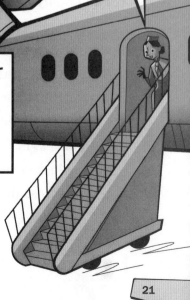

HURRY, MR. ELIZALDE!

ELIZALDE BOUGHT AN AIRLINE TICKET TO COSTA RICA, A COUNTRY WHICH HAD NO EXTRADITION TREATY WITH THE REPUBLIC OF THE PHILIPPINES. THAT MEANT HE COULDN'T BE RETURNED TO FACE JUSTICE.

THE GREAT SHAKESPEARE FORGERY

If you're going to go to all the trouble of stealing an author's name and creating a forgery of his work, you might as well steal from the best. Anyone interested in a new play by William Shakespeare?

THE PLAYERS

William Henry Ireland and Samuel Ireland

William Henry Ireland was 16 years old and really depressed. It was 1793 and he had recently been kicked out of school in London, England. His father, Samuel Ireland, was not happy about it.

William really admired his father, and had always tried his best to please him, but his father still treated him like a hopeless dolt.

Being kicked out of school was the last straw. Samuel Ireland decided to forget about further schooling for William.

THE OFFICE OF WILLIAM'S PRINCIPAL, LONDON, ENGLAND, 1793

YOU'RE BEING SENT HOME, BOY. WE'VE DONE OUR BEST, BUT YOU ARE, I'M SORRY TO SAY, INCORRIGIBLY STUPID.

HIS FATHER HAD ALREADY SPENT A LOT OF MONEY KEEPING WILLIAM IN SCHOOL, HOPING HE WOULD BECOME A RICH, IMPORTANT LAWYER.

I GIVE UP, SON. YOU ARE UTTERLY HOPELESS!

WILLIAM'S REAL PASSION WAS FOR BOOKS AND POETRY.

William's father apprenticed him to a local lawyer as a lowly clerk. He sat in the dusty office all day filing boring documents. His father's cruel put down was painful for William.

You might have thought that a man who sold books and absolutely adored William Shakespeare (like a lot of people, Samuel called him "The Immortal Bard") would have appreciated a son who wrote poetry. But Samuel just tossed William's verses aside. They didn't have the "true genius" of Shakespeare's, he said.

Samuel Ireland was so obsessed with William Shakespeare that he made his family listen to readings from Shakespeare's plays and poems every single evening. He'd even bought a chair and a purse that were supposed to have belonged to Shakespeare. William was pretty sure they were just stupid fakes.

Was William Shakespeare himself just a scam? There are lots of theories proposing that the real William Shakespeare, from a humble family in Stratford-upon-Avon, could never have written such brilliant plays. It must have been someone more educated and cultured, using a pen name, they say. One theory has it that the famous poet and dramatist Christopher Marlowe faked his own death to avoid criminal charges and lived on to write the works attributed to Shakespeare. (According to official reports, Marlowe was stabbed to death in a knife fight when he was 29.) Most scholars don't believe this theory, however.

THE SCAM

Samuel Ireland was puzzled. Why was so little known about Shakespeare's life? Why had so few examples of his signature or handwriting ever been found? How could a man become so famous yet leave behind so little evidence of his everyday life?

He suspected that someone had collected the Bard's papers long before anyone realized how valuable they would be. Someone was waiting to cash in. Samuel would give anything for just one signature!

That gave William an idea. What if he could make his father's dream come true? At work, William handled a lot of old documents—land deeds, mortgage certificates, and court records. He could also get his hands on some aged parchment.

WILLIAM BORROWED A COLLECTION OF SHAKESPEARE'S
WORKS WITH A PRINTED VERSION OF THE BARD'S SIGNATURE.
ONE AFTERNOON WHEN HE WAS ALONE IN THE OFFICE, HE STUDIED
THE SIGNATURE CAREFULLY AND THEN PRACTICED IT, AGAIN AND AGAIN.

HMMM. REALLY, IT'S NOT THAT HARD.

IT WASN'T LONG BEFORE IT BEGAN TO LOOK QUITE CONVINCING.

THE MYSTERIOUS "MR. H"

William consulted a printer's apprentice on what to mix into ordinary ink to make it look more aged. He rummaged around and found a 17th-century land title deed to use as a model. Then he carefully wrote out a deed for some land near London's Globe Theatre, where Shakespeare's plays had been performed. He listed Shakespeare as the buyer and a Michael Fraser as the seller. He signed Shakespeare's name with his right hand, Fraser's with his left, then pressed a wax seal on the parchment.

Of course, he still needed a good story to make his "discovery" believable. For this, he invented a "Mr. H." He told his father that Mr. H. was a client for whom he'd managed to find a long-lost, very important legal document. In gratitude, the man had allowed him to dig through an old chest full of ancient papers in his attic and take anything he wanted. Mr. H.'s only condition? That William swear never to reveal his real name.

AND THIS MR. H....YOU SAY HE HAS MORE OF THESE OLD DOCUMENTS IN HIS ATTIC? POSSIBLY OTHERS THAT BELONGED TO... THE *IMMORTAL BARD?*

YES, FATHER. WOULD YOU LIKE ME TO TAKE A LOOK?

A NEW DISCOVERY
Splendid beyond belief

His father's delight made William feel giddy and reckless. Over the next two years, he kept "finding" more and more documents of the sort his father prized. More letters, another receipt. He even found a "Confession of Faith" in Shakespeare's own handwriting, apparently written shortly before his death, confirming his allegiance to the Church of England.

Samuel Ireland thought this was marvelous, splendid beyond belief. He sent invitations to a number of famous writers and scholars—including the illustrious biographer James Boswell and two other well-respected literary scholars—offering them the chance to examine his treasures for themselves. These learned men expressed their congratulations in the most glowing terms. And when Samuel brought out the documents, there was a breathless silence.

William had often heard his father worry that Shakespeare might secretly have been a Catholic, and Samuel hated Catholics. In those days being a Catholic was an extremely serious offense, often punishable by death. So Samuel was overjoyed to see evidence that Shakespeare had, after all, belonged to the "right religion."

William never forgot that amazing night when three of England's most famous scholars and writers sat in his own living room, praising his work without realizing it. Yes, he'd always known he wasn't "incorrigibly stupid"—but maybe the very opposite was true! Was the opposite of "incorrigibly stupid" something like "real genius"?

William decided to test his theory a little more.

He told his father that Mr. H. had given him permission to search beyond the old chest in his attic. He was now allowed to explore Mr. H.'s entire house.

And sure enough, over the next half year a whole new bonanza of Shakespearean treasures appeared: a love poem from Shakespeare to his future wife, Anne Hathaway. Some books from Shakespeare's personal library, with his handwritten notations in the margins. Then a startling discovery: a letter to Shakespeare from Queen Elizabeth herself, expressing her appreciation of his literary achievements.

Samuel Ireland was almost beside himself with glee. Hadn't he said that sooner or later the Bard's papers would appear?

William laughed happily. Life could be very good.

Making a new document look old doesn't require high-tech methods. A piece of paper might simply be crumpled and smoothed out several times over, then dabbed on both sides with a wet tea bag or a cloth soaked in coffee, giving it an antique look. Once the paper is dry it will look convincing—though not convincing enough to fool an expert!

THE SCAM GETS BIGGER

Samuel Ireland felt these magnificent treasures had to be shared with the entire world. So he proposed they publish the entire collection under the title *Miscellaneous Papers and Legal Instruments under the Hand and Seal of William Shakespeare*. In the meantime, he would display the collection with great fanfare in his bookshop. The collection attracted a steady stream of customers, both scholars and ordinary folk, who came around to examine William's extraordinary finds.

Filled with a growing confidence, and lulled by the fact that nobody was challenging his forgeries, William now decided to tackle the plays themselves. Early in 1795, William announced that he had found the original manuscripts of *King Lear* and parts of *Hamlet*—written in Shakespeare's own hand! To Samuel, this was almost like finding parts of the original Bible. As he held the parchments reverently in his hands, Samuel wondered aloud whether William could truly appreciate how precious this manuscript was. The delighted Samuel Ireland lavished praise on his son and promised to publish his discoveries for the benefit of Shakespeare lovers everywhere.

A forger makes or alters or falsifies an object or document and presents it as a genuine one, *with the intent to deceive.*

THE UNRAVELING

At work, William was having more and more trouble keeping his growing forging operation under wraps. He'd learned a lot about how to make the documents appear authentically old. His office looked like a chemistry lab. Bottles of inks, acids, emulsifiers, and watercolors; paintbrushes, boxfuls of pens and nibs; many different kinds of paper and parchment; candles, sealing wax, ribbons, and erasing rubber.

Soon, doubts began to surface. One Shakespeare expert had examined the documents and announced that they were probably forgeries. He'd had his doubts from the start, but hadn't wanted to say anything until he'd made a thorough study of the matter. With all due respect to his colleagues, he felt they were letting themselves get swept away by the excitement. A drama critic weighed in with a list of puzzling errors and inconsistencies in the documents. Pressure was mounting to reveal the true identity of the mysterious "Mr. H."

Even the newspapers took up the debate.

A RECKLESS FORGER

Maybe William's self-confidence had now grown to the point where he felt his forgeries were good enough for him to get away with it. Or maybe he thought he could silence his doubters if he produced the biggest, most astonishing find of all.

William told his father that he'd found a brand-new, never before seen or heard of Shakespearean play. In fact, not just one, but *two* of them—*Vortigern and Rowena* and *Henry II*. But this time there was a catch. Mr. H. was not willing to let these plays out of his hands, and so had agreed only to let William copy them out by hand.

For Samuel, this was almost too much to handle. He urged William to make those copies as fast as he possibly could, and for the next four months William slaved over his five-act imitation Shakespeare play.

ABSOLUTE GENIUS!

REALLY?

WILLIAM HAD TO TURN AWAY TO KEEP HIS RELIEF AND PRIDE FROM SHOWING. FINALY—AN ORIGINAL WORK OF "REAL GENIUS"!

William's father made sure that the text of *Vortigern and Rowena* found its way into the hands of Richard Sheridan, owner of the Drury Lane Theatre. However, Sheridan wasn't immediately convinced of its authenticity. He found the writing a bit rough, and thought Shakespeare must have been very young when he wrote it. He offered to produce the work in his theater that April, but his manager and many of his actors suspected it was bogus, too.

Still, people talked about the play in pubs and taverns, at parties and public gatherings, in universities and colleges. Even the king was rumored to be interested.

When the play opened on April 2, 1796, every nook and cranny in the theater was crammed. William and his father, who were seated in one of the boxes, received repeated cheers from the crowd.

Minutes after the curtain rose, everything began to fall apart.

William had found the story of Vortigern and Rowena in the same history book that Shakespeare had often used for his plots. Vortigern was an Anglo-Saxon king who had murdered his way to the top—not unlike Shakespeare's Macbeth.

THE ACTORS HAMMED IT UP, MIXED UP THEIR LINES, AND CRACKED JOKES. SOON THE AUDIENCE WAS LAUGHING ALONG WITH THE ACTORS. ARGUMENTS ERUPTED AND FIGHTS BROKE OUT.

ALL FURTHER PERFORMANCES OF *VORTIGERN AND ROWENA* WERE CANCELED.

THE DOWNFALL
A confession

After the disaster at the Drury Lane Theatre, public opinion turned against the Irelands. Fewer and fewer people now believed in the authenticity of the Shakespeare documents.

Most suspected that the Irelands had been duped, but a growing number began to accuse Samuel Ireland of having committed the fraud himself. In public, Samuel defended himself vigorously, but in private he asked William more and more desperately to reveal Mr. H.'s identity, or at least arrange a meeting with him so all this confusion could be straightened out.

William was being driven deeper and deeper into a corner. Finally, he couldn't think of any other way to end this disaster but to confess the whole mess to his father.

So he did that. He told his father what he had done. He apologized. He said he had never intended for any of this to happen.

At first Samuel Ireland looked confused. He asked William what he was going on about.

William tried to explain that he'd gotten carried away when he'd seen how happy all his discoveries were making his father.

Samuel's forehead remained creased in puzzlement. Then his face softened. He assured William that this wasn't necessary. It was appreciated, certainly, but it wouldn't solve anything. The solution was for Samuel to meet Mr. H. and for the two men to sort things out. That was the solution.

Now it was William's turn to be puzzled.

The next day William sent his father a letter describing in great detail how he had gone about producing his scams. He even included some of his drafts and discards.

His father barely glanced at them. He called it all a pack of rubbish.

William tried to use his brother and sister, who both believed him, as go-betweens. It only made their father angrier. He called William "a vain and selfish ignoramus."

William packed a suitcase and left the family home for good.

THE AFTERMATH

The following year, William wrote and published a pamphlet entitled *An Authentic Account of the Shaksperian Manuscripts*. It contained a full and detailed confession, with evidence and apologies, including a full exoneration of his father.

Samuel Ireland published an angry denial and disinherited his son.

Unfortunately for William, the public sided with his father. No one seemed willing to accept that William was intelligent enough to have fooled so many scholars. They all blamed Samuel—who went to his grave four years later discredited and disgraced, still insisting the documents were genuine.

For a while, William kept trying to set things straight. In 1805 he published an entire book on the subject, entitled *The Confessions of William Ireland*. The book didn't sell many copies. Eventually he gave up trying and began writing novels instead—over a dozen under various pseudonyms—to give himself a fresh start. They were reasonably successful, but they weren't works of genius.

Ironically, William's most successful publication became a complete catalog of Shakespeare's works—which didn't include *Vortigern and Rowena* and *Henry II*.

WAR OF THE WORLDS
A MARTIAN INVASION

It takes talent to trick an entire nation, and this scam's mastermind earned lifelong fame for his efforts.

BREAKING NEWS: MARTIANS ATTACK EARTH!

On Sunday, October 30, 1938, people in the United States listening to their local CBS radio station around 8:15 p.m. heard this:

"We interrupt this program for a special bulletin from Trenton, New Jersey. At 7:50 p.m. a huge, flaming object, believed to be a meteorite, fell on a farm in the neighborhood of Grover's Mill, New Jersey, 22 miles from Trenton. The flash in the sky was visible within a radius of several hundred miles, and the noise of the impact was heard as far north as Elizabeth!"

The announcer informed the audience that CBS had dispatched a special mobile unit to the scene. Also CBS's commentator Carl Phillips was interviewing an astronomer at the observatory in Princeton about the significance of the crash, but Phillips would give a live description of the event as soon as he could reach the site.

After a brief musical interlude, Phillips apparently reached Grover's Mill, and radio listeners now heard a burst of static, then police sirens. Listeners were told that a growing crowd of spectators was pushing toward the pit, despite police efforts to hold them back. Some had driven their cars right up to the crater, illuminating it with their headlights. Inside the pit was an enormous cylinder. A strange humming began to rise out of the crater, and some spectators shouted, "Keep back! Keep back!"

Phillips's voice rose sharply: the top of the cylinder was beginning to turn! It appeared to be hollow inside. Someone yelled for people to watch out, that thing was red hot and they'd get burned! Then *clank*—a large piece of metal fell to the ground.

Now Phillips was reporting a figure crawling out of the cylinder—a huge glistening creature like a monstrous snake with one…two…three separate heads on waving tentacles, their eyes black and gleaming, their mouths V-shaped, and saliva dripping from their lips. He told the listeners that he was going closer, to investigate.

Next listeners heard that police were approaching the creature, waving a white handkerchief tied to a pole—a flag of surrender. They could only hope that the creature understood what it meant.

Phillips then reported another shape rising out of the pit: a humped, mechanical thing on metal legs. Suddenly a brilliant ray of light shot out and bounced against a mirror. It was a flame, cried Phillips, a huge jet of flame aiming straight at the crowd, turning them all into flaming torches! Radio speakers vibrated with screams and explosions.

Everything was on fire, Phillips shouted. It was spreading fast and coming his way! There were more screams, another crash, and an explosion that could have blown the cloth out of a radio speaker. Then, abruptly, crackling dead air…

After a few seconds, an announcer back at CBS apologized for the interruption. He regretted to report that CBS had just learned that at least 40 people had been burned to death in a field east of Grover's Mill. One of them was CBS reporter Carl Phillips. The state troopers were commencing military operations and helping residents evacuate their homes. The announcer added that CBS was handing its broadcast facilities over to the military, and a Captain Lansing was standing by at the scene to communicate with the public.

"TOTALLY UNDER CONTROL"

Captain Lansing assured the American public that the situation in Grover's Mill was totally under control. Whatever was in that pit was now completely surrounded. Eight battalions of infantry armed with rifles and machine guns stood ready to blast it to smithereens. Whatever these creatures were, he said, they wouldn't dare raise their heads out of the pit again. This was nothing more than a good chance for the troops to get a little target practice.

Lansing paused, then reported that something else was coming out of the cylinder. A shield-like thing, solid metal, rose higher and higher until it towered over the surrounding trees.

He began to panic. The thing was standing up, he said, rearing up on metal legs...

There was a rush of air and a thunderous blast that sounded like gasoline exploding. Then the radio transmission went dead again.

When the broadcast resumed, an announcer from New York had taken over, but barely suppressed his panic. He informed listeners that the battle in Grover's Mill was one of the worst military disasters in modern times. The strange creatures were part of an invading army from Mars; of the 7,000 fully armed U.S. troops who engaged the enemy, only 120 had survived. Dead bodies littered the fields, crushed by the invaders' machinery or incinerated by the death ray.

The invaders now controlled central New Jersey and had torn down communication lines from Pennsylvania to New York.

MARTIAL LAW HAD BEEN DECLARED IN
NEW JERSEY AND EASTERN PENNSYLVANIA.

THE PLAYERS
Orson Welles and a convincing crew

What over 5 million CBS radio listeners were listening to—though most didn't realize it—was a radio dramatization of *The War of the Worlds*, a futuristic novel about a Martian attack on Earth written by the British novelist H. G. Wells. The play's producer, Orson Welles, was only 23 years old but was already a veteran of American theater and had appeared on *Time* magazine's cover. Radio dramatist Howard Koch and Welles teamed up to adapt Wells's novel for American radio. The similar names were pure coincidence.

Welles was known for doing almost anything to make his productions gripping and memorable. He'd found *The War of the Worlds* fascinating but old-fashioned, so he changed the English locations to modern American ones and added modern features such as news bulletins, on-the-spot reporters, and realistic sound effects.

One of America's most prominent names in film, Orson Welles (1915–1985) directed or acted in over a hundred plays and films, including *Citizen Kane*, which many critics have called the best film ever made.

Writer Howard Koch agreed with Welles, and in fact he was concerned that the broadcast still wasn't going to be realistic enough. On the day it aired, Koch complained that the play sounded too unlikely. "Nobody's really going to buy this story," he insisted. "It's just too fantastical to believe."

OUT OF CONTROL
Word spreads throughout the nation

By 8:15 p.m., the phones were ringing in police stations all over the American northeast.

By 8:20 p.m., people were pouring into the streets. Sirens wailed and hospital emergency rooms swelled with people suffering from shock, hysteria, and heart attacks. Militia headquarters were swamped with calls from members of the National Guards. "When should we report?" they shouted into their telephones. "Should we come down right now?!" Hospitals received hundreds of calls from doctors and nurses offering to volunteer their services.

Traffic on all the main highways rose sharply as heavily loaded cars and trucks scrambled to get out of town. In Indianapolis, a woman ran into a church where a service was going on, screaming, "New York is being destroyed by Martians—it's the end of the world! I just heard it on the radio!"

HYSTERIA SPREADS

Even in the western United States, people were unnerved. In San Francisco, newspaper switchboards were jammed. Gas stations all over did a roaring business as millions of drivers filled their gas tanks as they prepared to flee.

All over the United States, people poured into the streets to watch the night sky for signs of the Martian attacks.

As hysteria spread, police started receiving reports of actual alien sightings. "Yeah, I saw them!" callers would say. "Spaceships, Martians! Thousands of them! You guys got to get out here fast!" Fire halls received calls about explosions—houses, streets, entire villages on fire.

Many people also armed themselves and began shooting at anything that looked even vaguely Martian—people, deer, trees, clouds.

Calls were flooding in to the CBS switchboard, and telephone operators tried their best to calm the callers down. "No, of course it's not really happening—it's just a play. Yes, really. No—didn't you hear the announcement at the beginning of the show? Yes, and there were two more during the show. Honestly! No, no, there aren't any Martians. It's just an adaptation of a ... it's just an imaginary ... it's just a ..." No matter how often they repeated them, their assurances didn't seem to have much effect.

NEW YORK CITY POLICE ENTERED THE CBS BUILDING TO STOP THE BROADCAST. THE ACTORS, NOT REALIZING WHAT WAS HAPPENING OUT IN THE REAL WORLD, MANAGED TO KEEP THEM OUT.

ON AIR

By the end of the broadcast, the hallways around the studio were crammed with police, reporters, photographers, and gawkers. Finally informed about the situation outside, a delighted Welles and his crew escaped out a back door.

It appeared that Welles's production had been every bit as gripping and memorable as he'd hoped.

OUTCRY
The public wants payback

The next day, the newspapers ran banner headlines: "Nation in Panic from Martian Broadcast." Many people were indignant at Welles's recklessness. "Radio ought to act promptly to prevent a repetition of the wave of panic in which it inundated the nation," fumed the *New York Times*. Iowa Senator Clyde Herring called Welles a "Hallowe'en bogeyman" more concerned about theatrical success than potential damage and distress. He called for a law to curb such performances.

But the *New York Herald Tribune* columnist Dorothy Thompson called it "the story of the century." "It has shown up the incredible stupidity, lack of nerve and ignorance of thousands. It has proved how easy it is to start a mass delusion, [and has] uncovered the primeval fears lying under the thinnest surface of the so-called civilized man." She didn't think Orson Welles ought to be blamed at all. In fact, she suggested he be given a congressional medal or a national prize!

Several hundred listeners sued the network for up to $50,000 for "mental anguish" and "personal injury." However, all of the suits were denied—except for a claim for a pair of black shoes, size 9B, by a man from Massachusetts who said he'd had to spend the money he'd been saving to buy those shoes to escape the invading Martians! Orson Welles got such a kick out of this claim that he insisted the man be paid—despite the protestations of CBS's lawyers.

COPYCAT CHAOS

CBS eventually apologized to the public, promising not to simulate news broadcasts within a dramatization when the circumstances could alarm listeners.

This wasn't the only time an adaptation of *The War of the Worlds* created a stir on-air.

In 1949, a radio station in Quito, Ecuador, broadcast the play with local place names and references. The station's artistic director even planted fake stories in the papers about flying saucers seen in the days before his broadcast. He did not, however, take the precaution of alerting his listeners to the fact that the broadcast was a play.

When listeners heard the production, hysteria broke out in the streets. And when people realized they had been deceived, panic turned to fury. A mob gathered in front of the station building, smashing windows and doors. Then they set the building on fire. The army finally stepped in, using tanks and tear gas to restore order.

Two broadcasts of the play in 1968 (New York and San Antonio) went off without a hitch, but a broadcast on Halloween in 1974 in Providence, Rhode Island, caused considerable disturbance and some lawsuits. A 1981 production in Germany barely raised eyebrows, but a 1988 production by Radio Braga in Portugal provoked such terror among its listeners that over 200 of them stormed the radio station after learning they had been duped.

THE AFTERMATH

Although Orson Welles went on to achieve celebrity status in the film world, his production of *The War of the Worlds* remains one of his best-known achievements. In fact, *The War of the Worlds* has never stopped being broadcast—despite (or perhaps because of) its tendency to produce panic.

Orson Welles would have approved. He never regretted the uproar his famous production caused. He said later in his life: "Every true artist must, in his own way, be a magician, a charlatan. I have always tried my best to be both."

THE PRINCE
OF HUMBUG

P.T. Barnum (1810–1891) was one of history's most notorious scammers. This was just one of his many schemes.

THE PLAYERS

A swindler, an elephant, and an adoring public

*O*n January 17, 1882, a shocking rumor began to circulate. In London, England, Regent's Park Zoo had sold Jumbo, the country's favorite elephant, to a circus in America.

When the park's Zoological Society confirmed that the rumor was true, the British public was outraged.

"Jumbo Sale Provokes Shock, Indignation," the *Daily Telegraph* announced. The zoo was deluged with angry letters and telegrams.

P.T. Barnum, who was born in Connecticut in 1810, showed a knack for sales and promotion early on. When he was only 12 years old, he started selling lottery tickets. At 25, he launched his entertainment career with a scam involving a woman he claimed was 161 years old.

The enormous African elephant, at 3.6 metres (12 feet) tall, the biggest in the world, had been a fixture at the zoo for more than 20 years. Couples had been photographed beside him for their weddings, and later on with their new babies.

The man to whom Jumbo had been sold—for the astonishing sum of £20,000 pounds (about $50,000)—was an American, the notorious Phineas Taylor Barnum, the owner of P. T. Barnum's Greatest Show on Earth, a huge circus that toured North America year-round in 48 extra-large railcars.

Barnum's plan was to have Jumbo transported to New York by ship. His agent, "Elephant Bill" Newman, had instructions to load Jumbo into a huge wagon-crate and haul him down to the docks for transfer into the waiting freighter.

But Jumbo had other ideas. Confronted with his wagon-crate, he would not get in.

THOUSANDS OF CHILDREN HAD RIDDEN AND "GROWN UP WITH" JUMBO.

COME ON, YOU OLD BEAST!

WHOMP!

JUMBO FLOPPED TO THE GROUND AND WOULDN'T BUDGE.

NO AMOUNT OF YANKING OR YELLING COULD MAKE JUMBO MOVE.

JUMBO THE LOYAL ELEPHANT

Newman even tried hauling him up by hitching him to another elephant. It was no use. Jumbo stubbornly lay on the pavement, his trunk flopping idly about his head. Nothing would make him change his mind.

"Jumbo Doesn't Want to Leave Us!" declared the *Daily Telegraph*. "Jumbo Loyal to the End," announced the *Sunday Times*.

Crowds of Londoners charged into the Regent's Park Zoo, thrilled by Jumbo's act of loyalty. They brought him gifts, flowers, and casseroles. One bride even brought Jumbo a piece of her wedding cake! "Jumbo belongs here!" they cried.

Could Jumbo be bought back? Someone quickly started a Jumbo Retention Fund, and thousands of children contributed their pennies. The British Parliament discussed the issue, and even Queen Victoria took an interest.

Alarmed, "Elephant Bill" Newman telegraphed his boss in New York:

> PUBLIC OUTCRY ABOUT JUMBO, STOP. UNSURE WHAT TO DO, STOP. AFRAID THIS MAY DELAY OR BLOCK JUMBO SHIPMENT, STOP. PLEASE ADVISE, STOP.

To Newman's surprise, P.T. Barnum replied:

> NOT WORRIED, STOP. LET HIM LIE THERE FOR A WEEK IF HE WANTS TO, STOP. BEST ADVERTISING IN THE WORLD, STOP. JUST MAKE SURE HE'S WELL FED AND WATERED, STOP.

BARNUM'S WIN-WIN BATTLE
The fight for Jumbo

Newman shouldn't have been surprised. This was the kind of attitude that had already made Barnum famous (and infamous) all over the United States. He believed that "a problem is just another word for an opportunity" and that "all advertising is good advertising."

To Barnum, any uproar was a good uproar, and any uproar at all was worth making bigger.

So the famous scam artist devised a clever plan. He secretly sent money to London with instructions to start up a Rescue Jumbo crusade. This group—not realizing they were being financed by the very person they were opposing—used the money to print flyers, take out newspaper advertisements, and stage protest rallies. The rallies got lots of newspaper coverage. Very good.

Then Barnum paid for a similar crusade in New York City. This group also printed flyers, took out newspaper advertisements, and staged protest rallies. These rallies also got lots of newspaper coverage.

Even better.

P. T. Barnum was often called the "Prince of Humbugs." Although we now use "humbug" to mean "nonsense," in Barnum's time, it was another word for "hoax." By the time Barnum bought Jumbo, he had been in the entertainment business for almost 50 years and had established a well-deserved reputation as a master of flair and deception.

A TREMENDOUS UPROAR!

Once the two organizations became aware of each other, things really heated up. More statements to the press. More letters to the editor. Protest marches. A tremendous uproar! From Barnum's point of view, this was getting better and better.

But Barnum was just getting started. He proceeded to pay several British journalists to urge the public to write protest letters. Soon letters were pouring into the office of the British prime minister, the queen's office at Buckingham Palace, the park's Zoological Society, and editorial offices of London's newspapers. The Society received so many, it had to hire extra clerks to answer them all.

What was the next step? Barnum began selling Jumbo souvenirs— Jumbo hats, Jumbo neckties, Jumbo prints, Jumbo earrings, brace- lets, fans, and trading cards. All the upset people coming down to the zoo to visit Jumbo for the last time became easy targets for Barnum's aggressive sales people. The profits started rolling in.

Jumbo didn't get up for almost two weeks. When he finally gave in and entered his wagon-crate, tens of thousands of Londoners lined the streets to watch it roll by on its way to the docks.

But even after Jumbo was safely housed in the ship and on his way to America, Barnum didn't let up. Every day, he telegraphed an update on Jumbo's health and activities to newspapers on both sides of the Atlantic. Journalists he'd paid himself were more than happy to spread the word.

And every day, Barnum's employees stuffed copies of these updates into rubber bags, inflated them, and threw them over the ship's side. Barnum announced that anyone who found one of these messages would win an entire day with Jumbo.

It's not clear whether anyone ever claimed this prize, but if they did, they may not have enjoyed it much. For, contrary to Barnum's splashy advertisements in the United States ("Jumbo—The New Darling of the American People!"), Jumbo was actually a cranky, smelly, badly behaved animal.

Many African elephants develop bad tempers after maturity, and Jumbo's was the main reason for the decision of the Regent's Park Zoo to sell him. He'd once almost destroyed his heavily reinforced house, and twice ripped his iron chains right out of their cement footings. He'd also injured several of the zoo's cleaning staff, and he regularly trashed his feeding bin and drinking buckets.

"THE GREATEST ELEPHANT IN THE WORLD!"

To calm Jumbo down, his British handlers had come up with the idea of feeding him whisky—and it worked. That was the good news. The bad news was that, over the years, Jumbo had become a drunk. It now took several bottles of whisky a day to keep him quiet. If whisky was unavailable, Jumbo would settle for beer, port wine, or just about any alcoholic drink. But all this drinking made Jumbo bloated, which meant he passed a lot of gas. According to Bill Newman, Jumbo farted "like a hero." He advised people to stay a good distance upwind of him at all times.

After 13 days at sea—which Barnum used to stoke Jumbo-mania in the United States—Jumbo's freighter arrived in New York. A huge crowd had been waiting for almost a day, entertained by Barnum's clowns and encouraged by Barnum's agents to buy more Jumbo souvenirs.

When 16 horses couldn't drag Jumbo's wagon-crate up the ship's ramp, hundreds of men joined in, and the wagon moved slowly up Broadway, all the way to Madison Square Garden, where the rest of Barnum's circus had been playing all month.

During the next four weeks, over half a million people shoved their way into the Garden to *ooh* and *ahh* over "Jumbo—The Greatest Elephant in the World!" Box office earnings very soon covered his entire purchase and transportation costs.

MONEY FOR NOTHING

Jumbo's American career

Over the next four years, and under Barnum's careful guidance—not to mention his massive, ongoing advertising campaign—Jumbo did indeed become "America's Darling." He became the main draw for The Greatest Show on Earth, helping pull in over 12 million paying customers from all over the United States.

There was so much hype, in fact, that no one seemed to notice that he was really just a very ordinary African elephant, who didn't even perform tricks like the other elephants in the circus. (African elephants were considered unteachable.) He just stood there, or walked in slow circles, while the band blared and the over-excited ringmaster bellowed out his star elephant's many supposed abilities and virtues.

Jumbo died late one night in 1885, when he refused to budge off a railroad track running next to the one on which his circus car was parked. He'd been having an off day and his handlers had fed him a lot of whisky. He was hit and killed by a passing freight train.

AFTERMATH

But that didn't mean he stopped making money for Barnum.

For the next several seasons, a gigantic version of Jumbo kept touring with the circus, amazing American children and fattening Barnum's bank account. Meanwhile, Barnum published *The Life, History and Death of Jumbo*—a biography of Jumbo so full of inventions, exaggerations, and outright lies that it could have been called pure fiction.

It was a bestseller for years.

THE IRREPRESSIBLE SHOWMAN IMMEDIATELY ORDERED A CREW OF TAXIDERMISTS TO TAKE JUMBO'S WRINKLY HIDE, STRETCH IT AS MUCH AS THEY COULD, AND STUFF AND MOUNT IT.

EXCELLENT!

P.T. BARNUM WAS VERY PLEASED. JUMBO LOOKED EVEN BIGGER THAN BEFORE!

INSTANT GLOBE CIRCLING— JUST ADD WATER

Before GPS devices, yachting race officials relied on sailors' reports. In this race, that was a fatal mistake.

A ONE-OF-A-KIND RACE

On March 17, 1968, in London, England, a great banner headline appeared in the *Sunday Times* newspaper. It announced the creation of a solo, nonstop, round-the-world *Sunday Times* Golden Globe Yacht Race—the first race of its kind and the longest, most challenging competition in the history of yachting.

No one had ever sailed single-handedly around the world without stopping at least once. The sailor who could do so in the fastest time would receive a prize of £5,000 (about $10,000).

The race was unusual in several respects. First, anyone could enter the race from any port north of latitude 40° north, so long as they circled the globe and finished back where they'd started.

Second, contestants could start their race anytime between June 1, 1968, and October 31, 1968. Everyone would have to keep an accurate daily logbook, which judges would examine at the end of the race. The prize for fastest time would be awarded after the final contestant had landed back in his home port. An additional prize—a trophy—would be awarded to the first finisher.

THE PLAYERS

The race attracted many of the world's most accomplished sailors, including Bill Leslie King, a British ex-naval submarine commander, and Robin Knox-Johnston, known for the speed of his ketch *Suhaili*.

Other famous entrants included Bernard Moitessier of France, British naval commander Nigel Tetley, Australian dentist Bill Howell, British adventurers John Ridgway and Chay Blyth, Italian yachting champion Alex Carozzo, and award-winning French sailor Loïck Fougeron.

Then there was a contestant completely unknown to the yachting world. He hadn't set any records or won any prizes. All that reporters knew was that his name was Donald Crowhurst, his home port was Teignmouth, England, and his boat was named the *Teignmouth Electron*. The press called him the "dark horse" entrant.

HE'D SMASHED UP THREE CARS BY THE TIME HE TURNED 26...

DRIVING A MOTORCYCLE DRUNK THROUGH A BARRACKS FULL OF SLEEPING MEN? WE WILL NOT TOLERATE SUCH CONDUCT, CROWHURST.

. . . AND GOTTEN HIMSELF KICKED OUT OF THE ROYAL AIR FORCE.

THE SET-UP

Donald Crowhurst was an electronics engineer who had entered the race completely on impulse. That didn't surprise anyone who knew him. He was a very unpredictable and reckless man.

Yet Crowhurst was also smart and charming and could make you feel as if you were the most important person in the world. As a result, he had a lot of friends.

THE NOVICE SAILOR
High hopes and confident claims

But even his friends rolled their eyes when they heard that Crowhurst had entered the *Sunday Times* yacht race. What on Earth could he have been thinking? Crowhurst barely knew how to sail—he was a novice sailor at best. And what was all this about a boat called the *Teignmouth Electron*? Crowhurst didn't even own a boat.

"That's true, but I'm going to build one," Crowhurst grinned. "And when I do, that's what it's going to be called."

That's when his friends began questioning his sanity in all seriousness.

To build an ordinary weekend sailboat from scratch in a mere six months—the time remaining until the October 31 deadline—might be possible. But to design, build, launch, test, tune up, and properly provision a boat for a race as grueling as the Golden Globe would take at least a year, even under the best of circumstances. It would also cost at least £50,000.

And Donald Crowhurst was broke.

YOU WANT MONEY FOR WHAT?

FINDING A BACKER
When the money you risk is not your own

It wasn't that Crowhurst didn't know how to handle money. Three years earlier he'd founded his own electronics factory, Electron Utilization, which grew to employ twelve workers.

But Crowhurst got bored easily, and he grew tired of running a business. Soon the plant was down to half a dozen workers, then only a single employee working part-time.

His main financial backer, Stanley Best, demanded a look at Crowhurst's finances, and while he didn't find anything dishonest, it was clear that most of his investment had been lost.

So Stanley Best was probably the least likely person on Earth to lend Donald Crowhurst any more money— but Crowhurst called him anyway.

STANLEY, I'M DESPERATE. I'VE HAD NO LUCK FINDING SPONSORS AND I'M RUNNING OUT OF TIME. COULD YOU BE A GOOD SPORT AND LEND ME £50,000?

Best's initial reply was probably unprintable, but somehow, after a series of urgent, pleading phone calls and long meetings, he agreed to put up £30,000 to build a bare-bones version of the *Teignmouth Electron*.

Crowhurst's friends pitched in, and the project, a 12.5-meter (41-foot) trimaran, began to shape up.

A trimaran is a boat with three hulls: a main one in the middle and a smaller one on each side, like outrigger floats. Trimarans are very fast and stable with a wind at their backs. But when the wind blows from the sides, they become sluggish and hard to keep on course.

Even with everyone helping, the work progressed at a frustratingly slow pace. Crowhurst worked 20 hours a day, negotiating, suggesting, fixing, inventing, and arguing with everyone. There were plenty of bungles—hatch covers that didn't fit, equipment that didn't work, sails of the wrong shape or size, and badly wired motors. Some things got fixed, but many didn't.

Five months later, when the team tested the *Teignmouth Electron* for the first time at sea, so many things went wrong that it almost sank twice, and the test trip took two weeks instead of the planned three days!

At last, though, Crowhurst and his team were satisfied that the yacht was sea-worthy—if barely. They were ready for the race.

ON OCTOBER 31, 1968, AT 4:52 P.M., ONLY SEVEN HOURS BEFORE THE FINAL CUTOFF, THE *TEIGNMOUTH ELECTRON* STAGGERED OUT OF TEIGNMOUTH HARBOR TO ENTER THE SUNDAY *TIMES* GOLDEN GLOBE YACHT RACE— WITH HER FINAL COAT OF PAINT BARELY DRY, HER CABIN STILL LITTERED WITH UNINSTALLED NAUTICAL EQUIPMENT, AND A STACK OF UNPAID BILLS FLUTTERING IN HER WAKE.

AND THEY'RE OFF

Not surprisingly, Crowhurst had a poor start. On November 2, he radioed a message to Rodney Hallworth, his press agent for the race, that the *Teignmouth Electron*'s self-steering gear was falling apart and an outrigger float was filling with water. On November 5, he radioed again: the generator had failed, and his batteries were running low. Then he sent no messages for almost two weeks.

When Crowhurst radioed again, on November 16, he had managed to fix his generator, but now crosswinds were slowing him down. He was just off the coast of Portugal, and sailing less than 50 nautical miles per day—the slowest sailing speed of any race contestant.

Finally, a month after setting sail, Crowhurst was far enough into the Atlantic Ocean to catch the northeast trade winds—winds that blew from behind and pushed him forward. The *Teignmouth Electron* surged ahead. On December 10, Crowhurst reported that he'd just finished a week of 145 to 174 nautical miles per day—including one day in which he'd managed a whopping 243 nautical miles.

He was now halfway between Africa and South America in the mid-Atlantic, with a 1000-mile sail straight down to the tip of Africa ahead of him and the wind at his back. On Christmas Eve, he reported he was already rounding the Cape of Good Hope.

Hallworth and the rest of Crowhurst's friends in Teignmouth couldn't believe their luck. They'd thought their boat was a total loser. And they were even more amazed to learn that Crowhurst's 243 nautical miles in a 24-hour period might be a world record!

Another factor that improved the Teignmouth Electron's position was the other contestant's bad luck. Ridgway, Blyth, and Howell had dropped out with mechanical problems. King lost a mast in a storm. Carozzo developed a stomach ulcer and gave up. Fougeron capsized and quit. Knox-Johnston capsized but managed to right his boat and was carrying on in the lead, his gear smashed and his sail in tatters. Only Tetley and Moitessier were still in good shape and sailing steadily, though neither was managing to match Crowhurst's speed.

DUPED!

CROWHURST DROPS OFF THE MAP

Crowhurst sent several more reports. Each time, his odds in the race improved. Then, on January 20, 1969, he reported more generator trouble. After that, only one more transmission came through, on January 21.

For the next three weeks, Hallworth sent radio queries to the *Teignmouth Electron* but received no reply. After another three weeks of dead air, everyone began to worry. By now, barring any significant problems, Crowhurst should have been somewhere in the Tasman Sea, sailing east between Australia and New Zealand, but no naval traffic was reporting him there.

And on April 2, to everyone's utter astonishment, the London *Sunday Times* received a letter from Bernard Moitessier, explaining that he'd had such a great time sailing through the South Pacific he was dropping out of the race to spend some quality time in the islands!

There was also no sign of Robin Knox-Johnston, until April 6, when a tanker spotted him in the middle of the Atlantic Ocean. His boat was a mess and his speed was very slow—but he was still sailing valiantly.

That left Nigel Tetley, who had rounded Cape Horn, the southernmost tip of South America, on March 20 and was now heading north, making a beeline for home.

Only Crowhurst remained unaccounted for. His odds in the betting shops of England dropped lower and lower.

ACHIEVING THE IMPOSSIBLE

Then, on April 9, more than 10 weeks after Crowhurst's last radio message, a very faint signal from the *Teignmouth Electron* reached England via a radio station in Argentina. Crowhurst was approaching Diego Ramírez, a small island just southwest of Cape Horn. This meant he had already sailed all the way around the bottom of the world and was now on the last leg of his return journey.

Not only that, but he'd been belting along at about 178 nautical miles per day. If he could keep that up, he might beat Nigel Tetley and win the race for fastest time.

To Crowhurst's team in Teignmouth this was incredible! One minute their man was dead last, then he was setting world records, then he disappeared completely, and now he was chasing the leader—how was this going to end?

On April 18, Crowhurst radioed that he'd rounded Cape Horn and was passing the Falkland Islands east of Argentina. The news sent Nigel Tetley's support team into a panic. Tetley's trimaran was damaged, and he'd been sailing slowly, hoping to keep it in one piece during the final month's sailing.

When they did the math, the Tetley team could see that Tetley wasn't sailing fast enough. If he couldn't do better than 140 nautical miles per day, Donald Crowhurst would win the race.

Tetley decided to go for broke. He strained his equipment to the utmost, desperately squeezing another 20 nautical miles per day out of his boat. At that speed, he might be able to win the race by a hair.

DUPED!

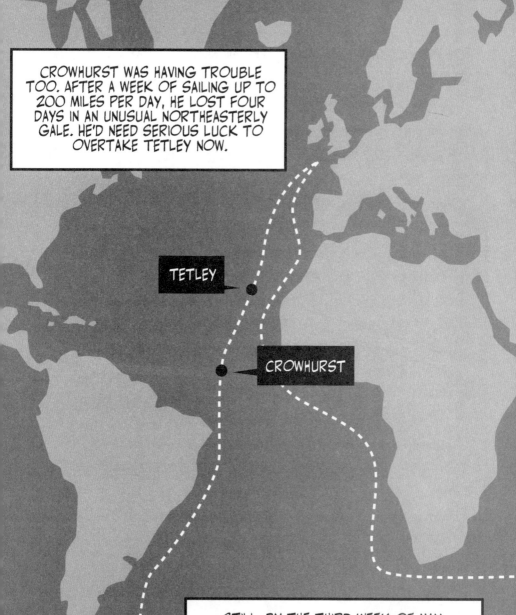

When Nigel's boat sank, all Donald Crowhurst had to do was drift the last 4,000 nautical miles back to Teignmouth, collect his prize, and spend the rest of his days awash in fame and fortune. The dark horse contestant was poised to win it all, and the world's news media went berserk.

But, oddly enough, Crowhurst didn't appear to be thrilled with his luck. His radio communications were much more preoccupied with all the mechanical and electrical problems he was having. Like Tetley's, his floats had been taking on more and more water. His steering gear was giving him endless trouble too, and his radio transmitter kept cutting out.

After June 1, Hallworth received no more radio messages from the *Teignmouth Electron*.

But this time the world didn't lose sight of Donald Crowhurst. He had crossed the Equator and was now sailing in the more crowded shipping lanes of the North Atlantic Ocean. Various freighters and ocean liners reported seeing the *Teignmouth Electron* as the trimaran moved steadily northward.

Piecing together the various reports, the race judges in London began to notice a strange thing. The *Teignmouth Electron* was sailing more and more slowly. Some days she was barely covering 20 nautical miles. In fact, Crowhurst wasn't even using his mainsail any more—just his much smaller jib.

CROWHURST'S REPUTATION GROWS

Then Crowhurst entered the Sargasso Sea, and that's when the *Teignmouth Electron* really began to slow down.

Now Crowhurst was barely making five nautical miles per day.

Hallworth and his crew weren't paying much attention to Crowhurst's affairs at sea because they had their hands full handling his affairs on land. So many offers and requests were now pouring in that Hallworth had to rent a second office, hire a secretary, and put in another phone line.

Officials at Buckingham Palace called on behalf of the Queen's husband, Prince Philip, asking whether Crowhurst would be willing to present the annual Duke of Edinburgh Awards next year. The post office called, offering to produce a special Crowhurst stamp. On behalf of the Teignmouth Chamber of Commerce, Hallworth had already printed 10,000 postcards featuring a photograph of "Donald Crowhurst, winner of the London *Sunday Times* Golden Globe Yacht Race," and was sending them all over the world. The cards read:

GREETINGS FROM TEIGNMOUTH, THE DEVON RESORT CHOSEN BY DONALD CROWHURST FOR HIS TRIUMPHANT AROUND-THE-WORLD YACHT RACE!

The Sargasso Sea is a strange phenomenon—a huge, eerily heaving expanse of floating seaweed in the middle of the Atlantic Ocean. It's also known for its calm weather—sailboats often have trouble getting enough wind to pass through all those weeds.

ON THE EVENING OF JULY 10, TWO POLICE OFFICERS ARRIVED AT THE CROWHURST RESIDENCE TO BRING HIS WIFE CLARE DISASTROUS NEWS.

EARLY THAT MORNING, THE ROYAL MAIL VESSEL *PICARDY*, EN ROUTE FROM LONDON TO THE CARIBBEAN, HAD ALMOST HIT A TRIMARAN FLOATING AIMLESSLY IN THE SARGASSO SEA. IT WAS THE *TEIGNMOUTH ELECTRON*, BUT DONALD CROWHURST HAD DISAPPEARED.

THE TRUTH SURFACES

120 NAUTICAL MILES TODAY, ROUNDED CAPE HORN...

DRIFTING AGAIN, NO SIGNIFICANT PROGRESS...

WEATHER NEAR CAPE HORN TODAY SUPPOSED TO BE FINE... WINDS NOT MORE THAN 30 KNOTS.

For days, the British and the American navies searched for Crowhurst. But when that mission proved unsuccessful, attention focused on the *Teignmouth Electron*'s logbook. That's when the answers began to emerge.

Investigators found not one logbook, but three.

Logbook #1 recorded a journey that went all around the world. Logbook #2 recorded a journey that was centered mainly in the South Atlantic Ocean. Logbook #3 was more of a notebook, containing freighters' radio reports of sea and weather conditions all along the route described in Logbook #1.

It didn't take the judges long to figure out what had happened. Donald Crowhurst had never sailed the *Teignmouth Electron* around the world. He had merely sailed into the middle of the Atlantic Ocean, then sailed in circles while reporting a journey around the world by radio.

Logbook #2 explained it all. Crowhurst hadn't originally intended to fake his journey, but by December 1, 1968, it had become obvious that the *Teignmouth Electron* was in no shape to sail the rough waters of the Indian Ocean and Tasman Sea. One good storm would have sunk it. Indeed, during his six months at sea, Crowhurst had once been forced to land on the coast of Argentina to make emergency repairs.

That's when the idea of a "virtual journey" had occurred to him. All he had to do was report fake positions along his round-the-world route, listen to marine weather reports from those locations, and incorporate those reports into a fake logbook.

Having believable entries was important, because Crowhurst suspected that his sailing speeds of 170 to 200 and more nautical miles per day, after his miserable 50 at the beginning, would make the judges suspicious. And he was right: one of the judges had already sent a letter to the race chairman, urging him to make sure Crowhurst's logbook was carefully verified.

THE INGENIOUS BACK-UP SCHEME

As the race neared its end and Crowhurst found himself neck-and-neck with one of the most experienced yachtsmen in the world, he became less and less certain that his logbook would fool navigational experts.

So he hatched an ingenious back-up scheme. He would not try winning the race. He'd arrange to come in second!

This would solve two problems with one stroke. Coming in second against one of the greatest sailors in the world was no shame. In fact, Crowhurst would still look like a hero. But a second-place finisher's logbook would probably not be examined very carefully. And that's what Crowhurst wanted.

Which was why, when Nigel Tetley's trimaran sank in a storm near the Azores, Crowhurst wasn't overjoyed—he was devastated.

As the winner, he would be unable to avoid the kind of scrutiny he feared—and its inevitable results. Shame. Dishonor. Humiliation. Disgrace.

As he neared the end of his journey, he sailed more and more slowly, frantically turning the problem over in his mind. What to do? How could he escape this looming disaster?

Finally, at 10:03 on the morning of July 1, in the middle of the Sargasso Sea, he felt ready to answer that question.

THE AFTERMATH

The race judges concluded that, at 11:20 a.m. on July 1, 1969, Crowhurst stepped off the deck of the *Teignmouth Electron* and drowned.

On April 22, 1969, Robin Knox-Johnston landed in Falmouth, where he had begun his journey on June 14 the year before. As the only finisher, he won the Golden Globe trophy and the £5,000 prize for fastest time. Knox-Johnson chose to donate his winnings to Crowhurst's family.

OPERATION BERNHARD

The most sophisticated and successful counterfeiting scam in history

THE SCENE: TRAUN LAKE, AUSTRIA

Early on May 13, 1945, a fisherman who had just left his house on the shore of Traun Lake came pounding back up the stairs.

"Wake up! Wake up, everybody! Come out here! You won't believe this!"

His half-awake family stumbled outside and gazed at the water in astonishment.

The lake was totally covered by a gently bobbing blanket of thousands of British banknotes!

Several other fishers appeared and a crowd gathered quickly. The air was filled with delighted shrieks, gasps, and exclamations.

"Where on Earth did this money come from?" asked a fisherman. "Did someone rob a bank?"

"And why are they British banknotes? Why aren't they Austrian?" another demanded.

"Never mind all that," someone else chipped in. "I just want to know—is all that money real?"

The question of real versus fake seemed easy to answer. Several people grabbed some bills and rushed over to the village bank. A cashier tested one with ultraviolet light and passed it around among her colleagues. Everyone agreed: the banknote was genuine.

Since World War II had ended only a week earlier, most of western Europe was under Allied military occupation, so a squad of American soldiers quickly arrived to control the situation. They roped off the area and tried to keep everyone away from the lake, but it wasn't easy. And despite the soldiers' efforts to scoop them all out, more bills kept floating to the surface. Eventually a fisherman suggested that the source had to be further upstream. He said the bills were probably being carried into the lake by the Traun River.

Sure enough, in the river the soldiers found a dozen wooden cases filled with banknotes, which had been flung into the river a short distance above the lake. The cases had burst and were slowly releasing their contents into the swift current flowing into the lake.

Then they made a second astounding discovery—an abandoned German Security Service transport truck about 20 minutes farther north. It was filled with 23 similar cases, all bursting with banknotes.

This was becoming too big for the local American commandant. He rang up U.S. military headquarters in Germany. Soon radio and telephone messages were flashing back and forth between Frankfurt and Washington, Washington and London. The FBI, Scotland Yard, and the Bank of England were alerted. Forgery experts from all three countries hurried to Traun Lake to investigate.

THE DISCOVERY OF THE ABANDONED GERMAN SECURITY SERVICE TRANSPORT TRUCKS SPARKED A 14-YEAR INVESTIGATION. BUT ALLIED INVESTIGATORS EVENTUALLY UNCOVERED OPERATION BERNHARD—THE BIGGEST BANKNOTE COUNTERFEITING OPERATION IN HISTORY.

THE SCAM

Winning the war with counterfeit currency

Operation Bernhard was first proposed to Germany's Fuehrer, Adolf Hitler, in 1939. It was shortly after Germany had started World War II by attacking and seizing Bohemia, Moravia, and Poland. In response, Britain, an ally of Poland, had declared war on Germany.

Instead of invading Britain, the German Security Service were proposing to flood the world economy with millions of fake British banknotes. Eventually it would become obvious that there were just too many of these bills circulating and people would realize that there were counterfeits in the system—but which were the real bills and which were the fakes? The currency would then be so suspect that it would be almost worthless. The British economy would collapse, and Britain would have to surrender.

Hitler didn't like the idea—he felt the German Reich (Empire) didn't need to win a war by using such "dishonorable" means—but he later agreed to a smaller version of Operation Bernhard. Germany's attacks on many more countries (including Holland, Belgium, France, and Russia), needed a lot of resources.

Germany had tried to invade England once before Operation Bernhard. In July of 1940, they launched an aerial bombing campaign known as the Battle of Britain. But by the end of October, when Britain still showed no signs of surrendering, Germany abandoned the plan.

THE PLAYERS

Bernhard Krueger and his counterfeiting crew

The man chosen for the operation—and after whom it was code-named—was Bernhard Krueger, the head of the Security Service's Forgery Division, which produced fake passports and other identity papers for Germany's spies. Unlike the other Nazi officials who ran the Security Service, Krueger was more interested in typography than politics. He also had a sense of humor, which some officers didn't appreciate.

Krueger was eager to get started, but there was an immediate problem: labor. To get Operation Bernhard rolling, he needed dozens of highly specialized workers—printers, composers, engravers, chemists, papermakers, banking experts. Trying to find people of this kind who weren't already fully employed in the war effort was going to be a huge headache.

The inmates of the Nazi political prison camps were not criminals. The camps were the Nazis' way of getting rid of anyone they considered politically unacceptable—homosexuals, Gypsies, political opponents, and especially Jews, whom Hitler blamed for all of Germany's economic troubles. Prisoners were brutally treated, forced to work long hours at hard labor, and kept on starvation rations. The death rate in the camps was staggering.

SEVERAL HUNDRED MEN VOLUNTEERED FROM THROUGHOUT THE CONCENTRATION CAMP SYSTEM, AND KRUEGER SELECTED 40 OF THEM. ABOUT HALF WERE JEWISH, NEARLY ALL WERE NON-GERMAN, AND ONLY ONE HAD ACTUAL COUNTERFEITING EXPERIENCE.

AND YOU SAY YOU WORKED 20 YEARS AS A PRINTER?

Suddenly Krueger had a brain-wave. He knew that some of the brightest and most accomplished scientists and other experts in the country were wasting away in the Nazi's concentration camps. Why not offer the work to them?

In his proposal to his bosses, Krueger insisted that his workers would have to be given decent accommodation, proper food, and a lot more privileges than was the norm. His superiors were appalled at the idea and grumbled about it for quite a while. However, since there was no other source of such specialized labor for Operation Bernhard, they eventually agreed.

Krueger gathered his chosen workers at Sachsenhausen prison, northeast of Berlin, where he built them a separately guarded compound, designated Block 19. It had heated rooms, washing facilities, and separate bunks for the workers—unheard-of luxuries compared to regular concentration camp conditions. Krueger probably wouldn't have been able to get away with civilized treatment of his men if Operation Bernhard hadn't been so top secret. Only he, Block 19's special guards, and the prison commandant knew what the inmates were actually doing there.

Most other inmates considered "Krueger's men" outrageously lucky. Most of Krueger's men felt that way too, but some had mixed feelings about their new jobs. On the one hand, they weren't as likely to be killed, starved, or beaten. On the other hand, working for Operation Bernhard meant helping the Nazis win the war.

The work they began involved an enormous challenge. British banknotes were widely believed to be impossible to forge. Their engravings were said to be too complex and intricate to duplicate. After the men had spent several hours carefully examining the various banknotes under a large magnifying table, Krueger offered to make things easier by having them produce only British five-pound notes.

Everyone was relieved.

THE SUBTLETIES OF PAPER

As well as the engravers, the papermakers were having problems, too. Krueger had sent several genuine banknotes to a laboratory for analysis, and the lab had sent back a list of the paper's ingredients. But when Krueger's men copied it, the bills didn't feel right. The paper felt too stiff.

Two weeks later Krueger's phone rang. "We've got it!" a paper-maker announced. The problem was the flax. The flax the British used in their paper came from Turkey.

Krueger ordered his assistant to get some flax from Turkey.

There was an embarrassed silence. "Herr Krueger—Germany is also at war with Turkey," the man said finally.

Krueger laughed. "How inconvenient," he said. "Then we'll have to smuggle it in. We'll get some through Italy. Or are we at war with Italy, too?"

The Turkish flax helped, but the match still was not perfect. After months of further research, the papermakers discovered that the British used recycled linen in their paper. So Krueger ordered his supply of linen cut into cleaning cloths and sent to nearby factories as rags, with instructions that the rags be returned after use and thoroughly washed, then added to the paper mix. That did the trick!

A third problem involved Krueger's method of aging the bank-notes. Clean, freshly printed banknotes are more likely to arouse suspicion than used, old ones. And engravings that remain sharp-edged are a clue the notes are fakes.

In an older banknote, the oils in the ink have soaked into the paper, blurring the outlines. After testing chemical combinations, Krueger found one that caused his ink to release its oils faster. This made his banknotes look several years old after only a few days in the dryer.

To age his banknotes even more, Krueger got half a dozen men to fold, crumple, and generally "work" the bills with unclean hands to remove their new look.

Finally, Krueger had to figure out how to number the bills. All banknotes carry a date, a letter and number designation, and the printed signature of the Bank of England's Chief Cashier at the time of printing. Krueger had to find out how many five-pound banknotes the Bank of England had issued during the past 20 years, what their designations had been, and whose signature they had carried.

It seemed like an impossible job—but the ministry's secret agents returned with the correct information in less than two months. Now it was all systems go!

THE TEST
Duping the Bank of England

Two weeks later, an assistant dropped the first batch of one hundred carefully dried, instantly aged, totally bogus British five-pound bills onto Krueger's desk.

Krueger picked one up reverently. He held it up to the light and examined it under his magnifying glass from every angle. Then he compared it to a genuine British five-pound note he kept in his desk.

"Perfect," he murmured contentedly. "This looks perfect. Now for the final test."

An agent was dispatched to Switzerland (which was neutral in the war) with a small bundle of the fake notes. Following Krueger's instructions, the agent approached a cashier in a large Zurich bank and handed her the bundle. He explained that he was worried that these bills, which he'd recently received from a client, might be counterfeit. He asked for her opinion.

The clerk asked him to have a seat.

When she returned a few minutes later, she cheerfully informed him that the notes were genuine. There was nothing to worry about.

"Are you quite certain?" the agent demanded. "I have reason to be concerned about this client's honesty."

The clerk assured him that she was quite certain. The bank had its own expert on staff, and he had inspected the notes personally.

But the agent sighed and pressed on.

THE SCAM SPREADS

The counterfeits were so perfect that the German Security Service expected to dump thousands of them into the economy at a time—and keep doing so for months or years. Also, Operation Bernhard planned to distribute banknotes all over the world. Soon Krueger's men were printing more than 100,000 fake British notes every single month.

Now what they needed was a trader who could keep up with that level of production. The job fell to Friedrich Schwend, a German who had once been an ordinary garage mechanic and was now a wealthy aristocrat, with businesses, mansions, yachts, and bank accounts all over the world. He operated on the premise that in any business deal, both sides should make a profit. This made him many friends and assured him a never-ending supply of customers. He kept agents in over 20 cities around the world, including Rome, Paris, and New York.

The purpose of counterfeiting banknotes is to trade fake notes for real ones. A counterfeiter might take fake British banknotes to a bank and trade them for genuine American dollars—or might use them to buy jewels, precious metals, or art for later resale. Most counterfeiters print as many banknotes as they think they can "sell" in an area, then hire agents to dump the entire print run fast, before the officials discover the problem.

Krueger asked Schwend how many banknotes he needed.

"Three hundred thousand," Schwend suggested. "No, five hundred thousand. I could use a million banknotes if you could print that many!"

Krueger said he'd see what could be done.

"And why bother with five-pound notes," Schwend continued. "Why not print fifties? It's the same amount of work."

"I'll think about it," Krueger replied.

The next day, Krueger ordered his engravers to begin work on a British fifty-pound note.

Krueger's men were now pumping out 500,000 banknotes per month in British 10s, 20s, and 50s.

Despite this, Schwend kept complaining that they were too slow. But Krueger knew that, if they printed any faster the quality would suffer—and if the quality suffered, the counterfeits would be detected and their agents caught.

Schwend's success wasn't surprising. It was now 1943, and Germany was beginning to lose the war, so fewer countries were accepting German banknotes for business transactions. In fact, despite Hitler's original instructions, Schwend often had to use the fake British notes to buy military equipment. Plus, with England recovering, the British pound was rapidly becoming the most sought-after currency in the world.

Schwend wasn't concerned about that. Their agent in Madrid, he told Krueger, had traded the fake bills for Spanish pesetas, then sent the pesetas to Lisbon to trade them for genuine British notes.

When the money got back to Schwend, he discovered he'd been paid in Krueger's own counterfeit banknotes!

"They're so good, even some of us can't always detect our own fakes!" he chortled.

Krueger had to call in some favors, but his men did eventually get their medals. Shortly afterwards, though, the camp commandant complained that the prisoners were wearing them very obviously as they came and went about the camp. It was upsetting the guards, who felt Krueger's men were thumbing their noses at them.

To keep the peace, Krueger asked his men to wear their medals only during the day, as they worked more privately in their print shops.

By the summer of 1944, Krueger's men were producing nearly 1,000,000 British banknotes per month. There were so many in circulation that in some countries, such as Yugoslavia, Bulgaria, and Romania, fake British currency had actually replaced the national currency. In Italy, many store owners quoted their prices in British pounds instead of Italian lira.

As Allied bombs destroyed Germany's armament factories, the Security Service used more and more of its counterfeit money to buy arms abroad. Schwend told Krueger that, for the best deals in weapons, he really should be printing American dollars. That would be the next hot currency. By January 1945, Krueger's men were producing about 10,000 American counterfeits per month—in addition to their British counterfeits!

TOO LATE FOR GERMANY

This had been everyone's greatest fear—that when all was lost, the Germans would smash everything, kill the prisoners, destroy the records, and flee. Fortunately, after a hurried argument, the soldiers decided the equipment was too valuable to smash. Everything would be packed up in boxes.

It took most of the day to load the trucks. They left just before dark in a convoy of 14 trucks. It was the middle of winter, bitterly cold, and no one had been issued a jacket or blankets. The roads were full of refugees and bomb craters.

After three days of almost no food or sleep, the convoy reached Mauthausen concentration camp in northern Austria, but there was no room for Krueger's men, and no rations to feed them. They were put in the camp's Execution Block, a freezing, windowless bunker, with walls pockmarked by thousands of bullet holes. That's where Krueger found his men six weeks later, sick and desperately hungry.

Krueger immediately transferred his men into new quarters at a nearby prison, where they were given heated rooms and cooking and washing facilities. Relieved, they began rebuilding their workshop.

Some opponents of Operation Bernhard, accusing Krueger of being a "Jew lover" (a crime punishable by death in wartime Germany), had gotten him reassigned without warning. It had taken him six weeks of struggling with the military bureaucracy to fight his way back to his men.

Only two months later the Americans invaded Austria. With enemy troops closing in and Krueger stuck in a meeting in Berlin, his second-in-command, Lieutenant Hansch, decided it was time to shut Operation Bernhard down for good. The men were ordered to pack up their workshop one last time. Then, according to strict orders from Krueger, they would receive their freedom.

When the last of four large army trucks had been loaded, army transports took the men to nearby Ebensee prison for a handover to the Red Cross. Two days later the Americans liberated Ebensee, and the men were freed.

Hansch and his Security Service trucks, meanwhile, disappeared into the night.

What happened next took inspectors years to unravel.

THE AFTERMATH

After traveling over steep mountain roads, one of the trucks broke an axle and had to be abandoned. A second truck—filled with counterfeit British banknotes in wooden cases—skidded into a ditch beside the Traun River. For some reason Hansch decided to dump its contents into the river. The remaining two trucks made it to a military research station before running out of fuel.

The engineers at the research station suggested wrapping everything in waterproof containers and lowering them to the bottom of a nearby lake, the Toplitzsee. When a witness finally confessed this information to investigators in late 1945, British divers searched the lake but found nothing.

Then, in 1959, a team of German divers found some of the waterproof containers. To everyone's amazement, they were still in perfect condition, and were turned over to the Bank of England. Recent dives have turned up more banknotes and Security Service records.

Operation Bernhard's counterfeit British and American banknotes were never officially withdrawn because they were simply too difficult to identify. This was a first in the history of counterfeiting.

Bernhard Krueger disappeared from Germany after he was accused of responsibility in the deaths of six of his men due to illness during his management of Operation Bernhard. The complaints were dismissed. Krueger returned to Germany in 1956 and died there of old age in 1989.

LA GRANDE THÉRÈSE STEPS OUT

This famous French scam artist cheated banks out of millions, but won the hearts of many.

A SERVANT GIRL WITH GREAT AMBITIONS

Thérèse D'Aurignac was used to being poor. Her family had never had much money. But she and her brothers and sister had long hoped for something better.

Her father had always told them that he'd been born into a very rich family, but his rebellious behavior as a young man had gotten him kicked out and disinherited. However, he said, his parents had promised that, if he married and made good, his children would be welcomed back into the D'Aurignac family after his death—and they would inherit a large estate. He promised that the documents proving this were locked in an old oak chest in his bedroom.

Thérèse was not convinced that her father's far-fetched story was really true, but when you're told the same thing day after day for 16 years, it's hard not to believe it, at least a little bit.

On January 5, 1874, Thérèse's father, René D'Aurignac, died. The moment had come, at last, to discover the truth. If Father was telling the truth, they could now retrieve the documents . . . and claim the inheritance!

THE PROBLEM OF CLASS
AND AN UNEXPECTED SOLUTION

Penniless, Thérèse, her sister, her two brothers, and even her mother became servants to rich families in the nearby city of Toulouse. Being a servant paid almost nothing, but at least they had food and shelter.

Thérèse felt hopeless. She wasn't a ravishing beauty, so there was little chance of marrying well. And her chances of promotion weren't great—in fact, she'd already been fired from several jobs for being too strong-willed.

The problem, as Thérèse saw it, was France's class system. If you had money, all doors were open to you; it didn't matter if you were a fool or even a criminal. But if you were broke, it didn't matter if you were a champion or a genius—the doors remained closed.

Then, in March 1881, Thérèse was in a third-class rail car on a train to Paris, to visit an aunt, when she saw an elderly American tourist in the first-class car fall out of his seat. It was exactly the way her Uncle Jean-Pierre had fallen off his kitchen chair when he'd had a "fit" years ago.

Ignoring the rule about third-class passengers not being allowed into first-class cars, she rushed through the doors and lifted him up, turning him over onto his side and keeping his tongue from blocking his throat, just as she'd seen the doctor do to her uncle. "This man needs to get to a hospital right away!" she told the porter who came running to help. "Can you get him a carriage when the train stops at the Gare du Nord?"

Thérèse spent the next three days caring for the man in his luxurious rooms at the Hôtel Grand Métropolitain. She prepared his medicines, fed him soup, and bathed his head and chest with cool water. He was extremely grateful and thanked her often, a welcome change from the way her employers treated her.

His name was Robert Henry Crawford, and he was an industrialist from Chicago, on business in Paris. He hoped that Mademoiselle D'Aurignac would be willing to help him recuperate until he was well enough to make the trip home.

He was so charming, considerate, and appreciative that she agreed.

Two days later at Le Havre, Thérèse helped him up the gangplank to his steamer and bade him goodbye. He kissed her on both cheeks, pressed her hands with great affection, and then pushed an envelope into them. He shook his head firmly when she protested.

"You've been absolutely wonderful," he said. "An angel of mercy and generosity. I will never be able to thank you enough."

She didn't open the envelope until she was back on the train to Toulouse. It contained 250,000 francs—more money than she had earned in the past two years. Enough money to free her mother from her servant's job and set her up in her own linen shop.

Two years later, Thérèse made an exciting announcement. She had received a letter, she said, from a law firm in Paris informing her that she'd been named in the will of the recently deceased Chicago industrialist Robert Henry Crawford.

UNEXPECTED FORTUNE
Thérèse's luck improves

Crawford's will bequeathed to Thérèse investments worth an astonishing 100 million francs! But there were conditions: that the inheritance be held in trust until she turned 30 and that she marry beforehand. If married, she would receive the money and interest on her birthday.

Suddenly, Thérèse was the most popular girl in town. The young men of Toulouse now didn't care that Thérèse was plain-looking and once a domestic servant from a poor family.

The marriage proposals poured in. Thérèse knew that these men were interested only in her newfound riches, but why waste the opportunity?

A YEAR LATER, SHE CHOSE FREDERIC HUMBERT, A LAWYER AND THE SON OF TOULOUSE'S MAYOR.

A NEW HOME AND BRIGHTER PROSPECTS

Thérèse's choice of husband turned out to be a smart one. Frederic wasn't at all like the strong-willed, ambitious Thérèse. He was quiet, easygoing, and a bit scatterbrained. He'd only become a lawyer to please his father. Whenever he could, he withdrew into his studio to paint. Frederic was perfectly happy to let Thérèse take the driver's seat in their marriage. He liked having a strong and decisive wife.

As soon as they were married, the Humberts moved to Paris, into a modest townhouse. But Thérèse had bigger plans. Word of her amazing inheritance had reached Paris, thanks to her father-in-law, Gustave Humbert. Gustave had taken a liking to Thérèse as soon as he realized that she was the "son" he'd always wanted. The two quickly teamed up on all kinds of projects.

It wasn't long before bankers were ringing Thérèse's doorbell, keen to lend her money. Anyone expecting an inheritance of 100 million francs was a pretty good credit risk from a banker's point of view.

And so, Thérèse borrowed money. Lots of money.

In those days, anybody who was somebody lived in Paris. It was not only the capital of France, but effectively the capital of all of Europe. Emperor Napoleon III had just spent almost 20 years cleaning and modernizing the city, and it gleamed with new and rebuilt palaces, bridges, monuments, and grand boulevards.

THÉRÈSE AND THE SOCIETY OF PARIS

Next Thérèse turned her attention to country estates—everyone who mattered in Paris had one. She bought two and a yacht that she moored in Le Havre. She filled her closets with clothes and jewelry.

By 1885, at the age of 27, Thérèse Humbert was well on her way to becoming an important person in Paris. Her salon was one of the most interesting meeting places in the city, attracting painters, politicians, writers, lawyers, and business people. Frederic ran for Parliament and won a seat. And the French president himself came to the Humbert mansion for dinner on several occasions.

Thérèse's rise in prestige was all the more surprising because she did not have a rich girl's education. She was plain-spoken and hard-headed, with a scratchy voice and a lisp. But people liked her sense of humor and curiosity, and that she didn't put on airs. She acquired a reputation for being lively and thought-provoking—and for treating her servants decently.

Teaming up with her brothers, she bought houses, estates, office buildings, and warehouses as investments. With Frederic's help she bought paintings—by El Greco, Velázquez, Daumier, and Toulouse-Lautrec—and invested in a number of art galleries (whose owners quickly developed an enthusiasm for Frederic's watercolors).

With the profits from her investments, she began to pay her debts. She also gave to charities and cultural projects. That raised her profile among Paris's politicians and social leaders.

A SHOCKING DEVELOPMENT

Then, in 1886, a story in the newspaper *Le Matin* announced that a challenge had been filed in the U.S. Supreme Court against Robert Henry Crawford's will by Crawford's nephews. They claimed to have found another will—undated—which included them as beneficiaries.

The bankers were alarmed—what if Therese did not inherit enough to pay back her loans? But Gustave Humbert, who'd recently been named France's Minister of Justice, examined the documents and decided that Thérèse had a very strong case. Calm prevailed.

Thérèse was furious. How dare these upstart Crawford nephews make a claim on her inheritance and threaten her business empire! She marched down to the law offices and demanded the inheritance documents. She would store them in her own safe, so those nephews couldn't get them!

THE FAMOUS SAFE

That safe in Thérèse's bedroom became famous among the bankers of Paris. It secured the inheritance against which they had loaned her, by now, over 70 million francs. They were as anxious to keep those documents out of the hands of the Crawford nephews as she was.

To make sure this remained so, Thérèse announced that she had hired a small army of American lawyers to challenge the nephews' claim. The nephews, apparently, did the same to challenge hers.

The case began to grind its way slowly through the American courts.

While all this was going on, Thérèse kept expanding her business empire. One of her biggest projects during this time was the founding of an insurance company with her brothers, Emile and Romain. Known as the Rente Viagère, this company sold life insurance, and like Thérèse's other companies, it received very positive newspaper coverage. (Being the daughter-in-law of the country's Justice Minister always helped to attract positive newspaper coverage.) Within a fairly short time it too was reported to be making a tidy profit.

No matter what sort of business she undertook, "La Grande Thérèse," as she came to be called, couldn't seem to fail.

The court challenge meant that Thérèse did not receive her inheritance at age 30. But even while the court case dragged on for over two years, no one seemed too worried. Two exceptions were Jules Bizat, an investigator for the Bank of France, and a banker named Delatte. Delatte was going to New York in a few weeks, so Bizat asked him to talk to the Crawfords.

DURING HIS TRIP TO AMERICA, DELATTE LOOKED FOR THE CRAWFORDS IN BOTH BOSTON, WHERE THÉRÈSE HAD TOLD HIM THEY LIVED, AND IN ROBERT HENRY CRAWFORD'S HOMETOWN OF CHICAGO.

HALL OF RECORDS

SORRY, SIR. NOBODY WITH THAT NAME HAS A REGISTERED ADDRESS HERE IN BOSTON. I CAN'T HELP YOU.

DELATTE SENT HIS REPORT TO BIZAT, WHO DECIDED TO CONFRONT THÉRÈSE.

I DIDN'T MEAN BOSTON, MASSACHUSETTS. I MEANT BOSTON, GEORGIA. THE CRAWFORDS HAVE LIVED IN GEORGIA FOR OVER 100 YEARS.

BIZAT FELT LIKE A FOOL, AND THÉRÈSE'S POSITION IN PARIS SOCIETY REMAINED SECURE.

THE ACCUSATION
A journalist demands proof

It wasn't until early 1901—13 years after Thérèse turned 30—that the journalist and novelist Emile Zola began writing accusing articles in *Le Matin* about Thérèse Humbert and her companies.

Most people reading *Le Matin* just grinned at Emile Zola's jabs. He was famous for making wild and unproven accusations. Thérèse Humbert shrugged and ignored him.

But Thérèse's chief attorney, Maître du Bruit, was taken aback, and he wrote a furious letter to *Le Matin* saying that Zola had done irreparable damage to his honor, and that if Zola was suggesting there was something suspicious about the Crawford will, he was prepared to open Madame Humbert's safe and let *Le Matin* or anyone else examine the documents.

When Thérèse heard about du Bruit's letter, she was appalled. She asked du Bruit what on Earth he was doing. She reminded him that she'd signed a guarantee that no one would open that safe or handle its documents until the courts had ruled on the rightful owner.

THE CHALLENGE

Du Bruit hadn't forgotten. He assured Thérèse that there was an article in French inheritance law that allowed for the opening of officially sealed documents if it was in the public interest. He was quite sure he could invoke that law in this particular case. After all, it wasn't only his honor that had been challenged by Zola but hers, too.

Thérèse didn't give a fig about her honor! She was afraid that opening the safe would jeopardize the Crawford court case in the United States—just when it seemed to be coming to a conclusion!

A TWIST OF FATE

When Thérèse turned to her various legal and political friends for help to block du Bruit from opening her safe, she found herself running into unexpected resistance. Zola's articles had been more effective than she'd expected. The prime minister himself, it was whispered, had now "taken an interest" in her case. He was said to be of the opinion that the only sensible way to resolve this issue was to open the safe.

A prime minister's "opinion" in France in the early 1900s had a lot of clout.

Two days later, a mysterious fire broke out in the Humbert mansion. It burned down a large part of the building's west wing, including Thérèse's bedroom. The bedroom was completely destroyed, but the firefighters said the safe was a fireproof model. They felt there was a good chance that its contents hadn't been damaged. The only way to make sure of that, however, would be to open the safe and find out.

The fire had given Thérèse such a case of jangled nerves that she packed her bags and told her staff she was leaving for one of her country estates. She told du Bruit that she was dead set against him opening the safe, and if he wanted to go against her express wishes and defy her express orders, she wanted nothing more to do with the matter.

The following week, on May 9, 1901, du Bruit, armed with a court order and surrounded by a crowd of bankers, reporters, and lawyers, instructed several workers to open the scorched and peeling safe. Since Thérèse had forgotten to leave behind her keys, the workers had to attack it with hammers and crowbars.

IN THE CHARRED REMAINS OF THÉRÈSE'S BEDROOM...

IT'S OPEN!

HER INVESTMENTS ARE WORTH LESS THAN 5,000 FRANCS!.

THE AFTERMATH

THE TRIAL THAT FOLLOWED, ON AUGUST 8, 1903, REVEALED THAT ALTHOUGH THERE HAD BEEN A REAL ROBERT HENRY CRAWFORD, OR SOMEONE LIKE HIM, EVERYTHING AFTER THAT HAD BEEN PURE INVENTION—COOKED UP WITH THE HELP OF EMILE AND ROMAIN.

It was soon discovered that Thérèse, her husband, and her two brothers had all disappeared. Within an hour, a warrant had been issued for their arrest. Four months later, they were all found in a boarding house in Madrid, Spain.

When news of the arrests spread across France, Thérèse became a folk hero. She had accomplished what most of France's citizens had only dreamed about doing: sticking it to the banks.

But even more, people admired Thérèse's spirit. She had confronted her poverty and lack of a decent job. She had rescued her family. And she had overcome her lack of beauty and her unpopularity, rising far beyond the social class she had been born into.

THE SCAM UNRAVELLED

The invention of Crawford's will was a way of getting Thérèse married and accepted into society. Its unusual conditions let her borrow from banks without having to produce her inheritance.

The condition of the money being handed over to her when she turned 30 was tricky, though. While it gave Thérèse 5 years to secure her social and financial position, it also meant that her scam would inevitably be revealed. Thérèse's plan was to become so successful by 30 that she wouldn't need the backing of the imaginary will.

While her investments were successful, they weren't nearly profitable enough to pay back the 240 million francs she'd borrowed, considering her lifestyle. She needed more time, so she invented some imaginary Crawfords to challenge her imaginary will. But it was still not enough.

It took the jury less than 24 hours to find all the defendants guilty. Their prison sentences, however, were lenient. Emile received only two years, Romain three, and Thérèse and Frederic five.

The crowd outside the courthouse shouted that she should be set free! As Thérèse and the others exited through a back door, with their coats thrown over their heads, they could still hear the crowd shouting and booing and throwing cobblestones out front.

Some say that the judge gave lenient sentences to avoid an appeal that might have caused an explosive scandal. It was said that Thérèse couldn't possibly have pulled off a scam that complex without a lot of inside help—from politicians, lawyers, and quite probably her father-in-law. No one else, however, was ever charged in "L'Affaire Humbert."

GOOD VIBRATIONS

Brilliant or brazen? Scientific scammer John Keely cheated supporters of a quarter-billion dollars.

THE PLAYERS

On February 17, 1874, the Rochester Room at the Fifth Avenue Hotel in New York was crowded with reporters. Their cameras were aimed at a cluster of strange-looking machines and gadgets bolted onto several platforms, and at the tall man trying to explain it all.

"What I'm going to demonstrate is something I call Etheric Force," John Worrell Keely said. "It's going to make every other form of power in this world obsolete. It is more powerful than any explosive known to man. But most amazing of all—this force can be harnessed using nothing more expensive than ordinary water!"

Most of the reporters looked doubtful. Keely had no reputation as an inventor, and he'd always been vague about his credentials. The newspapers were interested only because a very famous scientist, the German astronomer Johannes Kepler, had prophesied a similar "force" in 1625, and Keely was claiming that he'd finally found it.

If Keely noticed the reporters' doubts, he gave no sign. He went on to describe the engine he was developing: it would require no more than a single liter (quart) of water to drive a 30-car train from New York to San Francisco at 120 kilometers (75 miles) per hour.

"I'll believe that when I see it," one of the reporters jeered.

Keely led the group to a platform on which he had mounted a large brass globe filled with wires, tubes, and disks. He explained that this was a "shifting resonator," which activated the "vibrational energy" in the water. This energy was then passed through a "vibratory liberator-transmitter," which in turn drove his "hydra-pneumatic pulsating-vacuum engine."

"Why can't you use ordinary English?" a reporter complained. "I can't understand a word you're saying."

Keely said that his concept was so new that words hadn't been invented for it—so he'd made them up. He apologized for the difficulty. "But I think you'll have no trouble understanding this," he said.

He picked up a small glass of water and poured it into the resonator. Then he switched on both the resonator and the transmitter. They hummed quietly. He picked up a tuning fork and struck it, producing a strong, clear hum. Then he held the humming fork close to the resonator.

WITH A VICIOUS HISS, THE RESONATOR'S MOTOR STARTED TO SPIN VERY FAST. THE SOUND INCREASED TO A FRIGHTENING HOWL.

Next, Keely pointed to a length of thick, steel industrial cable fastened between two enormous iron buckles. Then he threw the lever on a huge hydraulic piston and quickly stepped back.

There was a scary-sounding twang as the cable became so rigid it started to vibrate.

Keely ducked, gesturing for everyone to cover their heads.

THERE WAS A SUDDEN BRIEF DROP IN THE HOWL OF THE MOTOR, AND INDIVIDUAL WIRES OF STEEL CABLE BEGAN TO SNAP WITH SMALL, SHARP EXPLOSIONS. THEN, AN INSTANT LATER...

BANG!

THE POWER OF THE ETHERIC FORCE

After the explosion, Keely groped his way through the haze and switched off the resonator, and the awful howl of the motor slowly died away. As the dust cleared, the reporters straightened and shook bits of blackened metal off their clothes. Some had dropped their notebooks and cameras in fright.

"And that," Keely said, "is merely a very small demonstration of the amazing power of Etheric Force. Good day, gentlemen!"

The headlines in New York's newspapers the next morning were everything Keely had hoped for: "Etheric Force Power of Tomorrow." "Simple Tap Water Will Power Trains, Ships."

> Machines in the 1870s ran on steam, a very dirty form of power. You had to burn a lot of coal or wood to make steam, and that produced soot and ashes that covered everything nearby. A new form of power that used only water and produced no smoke at all would be a truly fantastic development.

By noon, his hotel message box was bulging with telegrams. Everybody wanted to see how a few cups of water could drive an entire freight train from New York to San Francisco!

Keely patiently demonstrated his Etheric Force again and again. Sometimes his motor snapped pieces of industrial cable. Sometimes it twisted iron bars into pretzels. Every time, his spectators were enormously impressed.

It wasn't long before Keely was meeting with some of the richest businessmen in the United States. They all assembled at his small machine shop on North 20th Street in Philadelphia.

Those interested in Keely's invention included Charles Franklin, head of the Cunard Steamship Line, Henry Sergeant, president of the Ingersoll Rock Drill Company, John Cisco, head of the Cisco National Bank, and the famously rich John Jacob Astor.

They wanted to know whether he had taken out a patent on his idea, and whether he would consider teaming up with other inventors, such as Thomas Edison, who was working on an electric lamp. If Etheric Force could produce electric light, its possibilities were endless!

"Gentlemen, gentlemen," Keely responded. "The answer to both questions is no. I know nothing about business, and I have no interest in it. I simply wish to continue my research. To register a patent, or work with other scientists, I would have to share the details of my discovery, and I cannot take that chance. I am not prepared to lose my years of work—not to mention the potential profits."

His listeners had all heard of dishonest inventors stealing other people's discoveries. And Keely's discovery could be worth a lot.

One of the businessmen suggested that Keely set up his own company, with support from investors. Research was expensive, but with investors backing him, Keely could improve and speed up his research. "I believe I speak for all the gentlemen present when I say that we'd be interested in making an investment in such a company," he said.

THE BEGINNING OF
THE KEELY MOTOR COMPANY

The Keely Motor Company was incorporated on March 15, 1874. Keely's investors, who became the company's directors, paid him an astounding $15 million for half of his company's shares.

For the next three years, John Keely worked away in his machine shop. No one knew what he was doing in there because he always kept his doors locked.

KEELY NEVER EXPLAINED THE CAUSE OF THE EXPLOSIONS IN HIS MACHINE SHOP.

BOOM!

PROMISES, PROMISES

Keely assured the directors that he'd been working on just such a motor for the past three years, and he'd be ready to demonstrate it in public in three months, on July 1. It would power a circular saw, using five drops of water to cut ten cords of wood.

But on June 29, 1877, John Keely sent his directors a cancellation telegram.

POSTAL TELEGRAPH   COMMERCIAL CABLES

TELEGRAM

transmits and delivers this message subject to the terms and conditions printed on the back of this blank.

Telegraph-Cable
COUNTER NUMBER.   TIME FILED.   CHECK.
                              M

Send the following message, without repeating, subject to the terms and conditions printed on the back hereof, which are hereby agreed to.

REGRET TO INFORM THAT I HAVE ENCOUNTERED PROBLEMS HAR-MONIZING NEGATIVE AND POSITIVE VIBRATIONS OF MOTOR'S MAIN SHAFT, STOP. MUST POSTPONE DEMONSTRATION TO A FUTURE DATE, STOP. WILL BE IN TOUCH SOON, STOP.

"Negative and positive vibrations—what on Earth is that supposed to mean?" a director demanded. None of the others had a clue.

They didn't hear from Keely again for over six months.

Finally, they received a note explaining that he had abandoned work on his Etheric Force engine because he had discovered a newer, more powerful and efficient form of energy—something he was calling "Vibratory Sympathy."

SILENCE AND EXPECTATION

Now Keely was working on a powerful motor to harness the Vibratory Sympathy energy, and it was almost finished. He would demonstrate it in three months, on March 1, 1878.

But no one heard from John Keely on March 1, 1878.

They didn't hear from him on March 1, 1879, either—despite several queries and reminders.

THE BEAUTY OF VIBRATORY SYMPATHY WAS THAT
IT WAS BASED ON THE SIMPLE FACT THAT
EVERYTHING ON EARTH VIBRATES. TO TAP INTO
THIS HUGE ENERGY FORCE, YOU DIDN'T NEED
RESONATORS, TRANSMITTERS, OR EVEN WATER.
ALL YOU HAD TO DO WAS FIND THE RIGHT
COMBINATION OF MUSICAL NOTES.

KEELY GOES TO COURT

On March 1, 1880, the directors of the Keely Motor Company ran out of patience. They sued Keely in court, demanding that he hand over any of his inventions that might have commercial value, and to force him to explain to an audience of engineers or mechanics just exactly what he had been working on in his machine shop for the past six years.

The suit made headlines throughout the American northeast. In court, Keely admitted that he hadn't yet been able to produce a motor that could be used commercially, but that he was very close. He fully expected to be ready to test his latest prototype—a monster motor that could produce 25,000 horsepower using only vibratory attraction and musical notes as its source of power—by June 1, 1880.

He also agreed to try to explain his newest discoveries to an audience of experts. But he warned the judge that even mechanical specialists might find his ideas hard to understand.

He was certainly right about that. Everyone seemed quite intrigued when Keely activated a small test motor by playing mysterious notes on a violin, but after half an hour of listening to him explaining how this machine "diverted the polar current of apergy quite independent of centrifugal action," most threw up their hands and headed for the door. The few who stayed behind asked to have a closer look at the motor, but Keely absolutely refused to let anyone touch it.

KEELY'S NEW FAN

Afterward, three audience members met at a nearby café. One was a professor of physics, John Leidy; another was a physicist named James Wilcox; and the third was a poet named Clara Bloomfield-Moore, the widow of a rich Philadelphia industrialist.

Leidy and Wilcox were Keely supporters, but his performance had left them worried. By now Keely had spent over $60 million of his investors' money, almost bankrupting the company. Leidy thought that Keely was a decade or more ahead of his time—after all, scientists were only just beginning to learn how to use the universe's energy. But he suspected that the Keely Motor Company's directors wouldn't wait that long for results.

"What do you think, Clara?" Leidy asked. "You haven't said a word all night."

A MOTOR THAT'S ACTIVATED BY MUSICAL NOTES? I LOVE IT! IN FACT, I'M GOING TO INVEST MY OWN MONEY IN THE KEELY MOTOR COMPANY.

GENIUS...OR CRACKPOT?

Reaction in the press to Clara Bloomfield-Moore's $8 million rescue of the Keely Motor Company was mixed. The *New York Home Journal* praised her courageous support of scientific research, while *Scientific American* magazine suggested she was throwing her money away.

Clarence, Clara's son, demanded to know what his mother was doing, squandering his inheritance. Clara replied that she wasn't dead yet, and how she spent her money was her own business. Clarence disagreed. He filed a lawsuit against her, claiming she was a well-meaning but ignorant woman who had fallen under the influence of a scam artist. He lost the suit. The two didn't speak to each other for the next fifteen years.

Clara Bloomfield-Moore became John Keely's most loyal supporter and defender. She wrote enthusiastic articles about him in popular magazines such as *Lippincott's* and the *New York Home Journal*. She hosted elegant parties to introduce him to scientists who might become his supporters, too. She became the only person Keely allowed to wander around his machine shop.

Eventually, she wrote an entire book about Keely's work, entitled *Keely and His Discoveries*. Like Keely's lectures, it was so hard to understand that *Scientific American* called it all a bunch of incomprehensible nonsense. Keely, however, said the lady had got it exactly right.

A COURT ORDER

Keely's board of directors really didn't care. They just wanted Keely to hurry up and produce that 25,000 horsepower engine! It was now 1887, and they still had absolutely nothing to show for their investment—which had risen to almost $100 million!

It was time to take Keely to court again. After all, the only time they'd ever gotten him to cooperate was when they'd used that approach. If they could get the court to order Keely to hand over his test machines, they could hire a real engineer to unpuzzle the technology and build them a commercially salable version.

Hauled into court a second time, Keely was ordered by the judge to comply with his directors' demands. This time Keely refused outright. The judge ordered Keely to be arrested.

When two sheriffs arrived at Keely's machine shop to take him away, they couldn't get in. All the doors and windows were locked. "Open up!" one of them shouted. "Open up in the name of the law!"

There was no answer, but suddenly there was a terrible banging and smashing. Metal crashing into metal. Bursts of glass, and something that sounded like explosions.

A SCHEME IN RUINS

Inside the shop, it looked as if a bomb had exploded. Everything was smashed to pieces. Shattered glass lay everywhere. And on the floor, in a mangled heap, were the remains of Keely's test machines.

The sheriffs called in several men with a cart to haul the mangled machines away. "We think there may have been 11 machines," the sheriffs reported to the judge. "But it could have been as many as 15. There were so many pieces, it was impossible to tell."

Keely spent three days in jail before Clara's lawyers could bail him out. He was a model prisoner, quiet and cooperative.

The engineers who were hired by the Keely Motor Company couldn't make any sense at all of Keely's machines. They were simply too smashed up to reconstruct.

Faced with the possible loss of $100 million, the directors made a deal with Keely. The inventor promised to rebuild his machines, take out proper patents, and produce a motor within five years. In return, the directors agreed to find additional investors to keep the Keely Motor Company afloat for another decade.

Eleven years later, after rebuilding his shop and some machinery, Keely announced that he had found a way to "vitalize" disks made of a mysterious new metal, which, when "activated" with the proper musical sounds and installed in a special engine, could produce 250 horsepower of "vibratory thrust" for an entire day on a single charge.

Then he announced that he had discovered a way to use his vitalized disks to get airships off the ground and flying without using huge airbags full of helium gas.

THE PROMISE OF VITALIZATION

Finally, in 1898, Keely announced that his "vitalizing" process could fire cannons without gunpowder. He demonstrated by firing a test cannonball clean through a thick wooden beam, using only a cylinder that had been "vitalized" by a harmonica's sound. The demonstration impressed both military officials and Keely's directors—especially the new ones who hadn't seen his demonstrations before. The value of Keely Motor Company stock rose for the first time in 15 years.

But he still hadn't filed any patents or produced a marketable motor.

THAT WAS THE LAST THING JOHN WORRELL KEELY EVER SAID TO HIS MOST LOYAL AND ENTHUSIASTIC SUPPORTER. TWO WEEKS LATER HE WAS DEAD OF PNEUMONIA.

THE AFTERMATH

Immediately after Keely's death, a riot broke out in front of the Keely Motor Company's offices. Investors, reporters, friends, and enemies rushed into Keely's machine shop, grabbing machinery, equipment, papers, models—anything that might contain the secret of Keely's mysterious energy source. For the next several weeks, they tried to piece it all together, but without success. No one ever found enough parts to assemble an entire model or test machine.

The Keely Motor Company was declared bankrupt. John Keely had convinced dozens of America's most sophisticated investors to give him over a quarter of a billion dollars—without ever producing a single patent or marketable product!

But the story didn't end there. Clarence Moore, Clara's son, rented Keely's old machine shop, determined to get to the bottom of his secret. It wasn't long before he discovered something odd: the door to the shop had been shortened, and another step added to the entrance stair.

FIVE HOURS LATER, MOORE WAS HOT ON THE TRAIL OF KEELY'S TWENTY-FOUR-YEAR SECRET.

A SECRET UNEARTHED

What Moore found was a false floor, and between the false and the original floor was a network of pipes leading down to the basement. In the basement, he found a huge steel globe buried deep in the dirt. It weighed more than 3,000 kilograms (3 tons) and was obviously a pressure tank, fitted with connections for a compressor.

So the force that had driven Keely's mysterious motors was nothing more than compressed air! It was a technology as old and well-known as steam power, and certainly no improvement over it. Yes, it could generate a huge amount of energy, but you still had to burn wood or coal to produce it. Keely had hidden spring valves under the floor, so he could start his motors by pressing his foot down on a particular spot. Playing music had just been a method of distracting attention away from his foot! Keely's scam was exposed.

After the uproar died down, some people wondered if Keely's scam had been a cover for his real research. He'd spent day and night in his machine shop, and it couldn't have taken him 24 years to build a few fake test motors that operated on compressed air. Some people suggested that Keely had simply cooked up his fake demonstrations to attract enough investment money to pay for the research he was really interested in—a form of energy so advanced that he couldn't possibly have hoped to master it in his own lifetime.

FURTHER READING

Acer, David. *Gotcha!* Toronto: Kids Can Press, 2008.

Farquhar, Michael. *A Treasury of Deception: Liars, Misleaders, Hoodwinkers and the Extraordinary True Stories of History's Greatest Hoaxes, Fakes and Frauds.* New York: Penguin, 2005.

Innes, Brian. *Fakes & Forgeries: The True Crime Stories of History's Greatest Deceptions: The Criminals, the Scams and the Victims.* Pleasantville, NY: Readers Digest, 2005.

Pascoe, Elaine. *Fooled You! Fakes and Hoaxes Through the Years.* New York: Henry Holt & Co., 2005.

Stein, Gordon, and Marie J. MacNee. *Scams, Shams and FlimFlams: From King Tut to Elvis Lives.* Detroit: U.X.L, 1994.

Wilker, Josh. *Classic Cons and Swindles.* New York: Chelsea House, 1997.

BIBLIOGRAPHY

The Tasaday: Stone Age Cave-dwellers of the Philippines

"First Glimpse of a Stone Age Tribe." *National Geographic Magazine*, Dec. 1971.

"Anthropologists Debate Tasaday Hoax Evidence." *Science* Magazine, vol. 246: Dec. 1989.

Nance, John. *The Gentle Tasaday: A Stone Age People in the Philippine Rain Forest*. New York: Harcourt Brace Jovanovich, 1975.

The Great Shakespeare Forgery

Moss, Norman. *The Pleasures of Deception*. New York: Reader's Digest Press, 1977.

Ireland, William. *An Authentic Account of the Shaksperian Manuscripts*. Published online at http://newark.rutgers.edu/~jlynch/Texts/ireland.html

Blundell, Nigel. *The World's Greatest Crooks and Conmen*. London: Hamlyn Press, 1991.

War of the Worlds: A Martian Invasion

Bulgatz, Joseph. *Ponzi Schemes, Invaders from Mars and More Extraordinary Popular Delusions and the Madness of Crowds*. New York: Harmony Books, 1992.

Hadley, Cantrill. *The Invasion from Mars*. Princeton: Princeton University Press, 1982.

www.sacred-texts.com/ufo/mars/wow.htm

The Prince of Humbug

Saxon, A.H. *P.T. Barnum: The Legend and the Man*. New York: Columbia University Press, 1989.

Sifakis, Carl. *Hoaxes and Scams*. New York: Facts on File, 1993.

Sommer, Robin Langley. *Great Cons and Con Artists*. London: Bison Books, 1994.

www.well.com/user/kafclown/barnum/humbugs.html

Instant Globe-Circling—Just Add Water

Tomalin, Nicholas and Ron Hall. *The Strange Last Voyage of Donald Crowhurst*. Camden, Maine: International Marine/Ragged Mountain Press, 1970.

Roberts, David. *Great Exploration Hoaxes*. San Francisco: Sierra Club Books, 1982.

Operation Bernhard

Pirie, Anthony. *Operation Bernhard*. London: Cassell & Co., 1961.

www.scrapbookpages.com/Sachsenhausen/counterfeit.html

La Grande Thérèse Steps Out

Klein, Alexander. *Grand Deception*. New York: J.P. Lippincott, 1955.

Wade, Carlson. *Great Hoaxes and Famous Imposters*. New York: Jonathan David Publishers, 1976.

Larsen, Egon. *The Deceivers*. London: John Baker, 1966.

Good Vibrations

Klein, Alexander. *Grand Deception*. New York: J.P. Lippincott, 1955.

McDougal, Curtis. *Hoaxes*. New York: Dover Publications, 1958.

www.lhup.edu/~dsimanek/museum/keely/keely.htm

INDEX

Astor, John Jacob, 136

Bank of England, 101–103
Barnum, Phineas Taylor, 56–57, 59–60, 62–63, 67–69
Best, Stanley, 74, 75
Bizat, Jules, 124–125
Blit, 18
Block 18, 107
Block 19, 98
Bloomfield-Moore, Clara, 142–143, 146–147
Bloomfield-Moore, Clarence, 143, 148–149
Blyth, Chay, 71, 78
Boswell, James, 27, 28

Carozzo, Alex, 71, 78
Cisco, John, 136
Crawford, Robert Henry, 118–119, 123–127, 130–131
Crowhurst, Clare, 85
Crowhurst, Donald, 71–75, 77–81, 83–89

D'Aurignac, Emile, 115, 124, 130, 131
D'Aurignac, René, 114–115
D'Aurignac, Romain, 115, 124, 130, 131
D'Aurignac, Thérèse, 114–131
Delatte, Monsieur, 124–125
Diego Ramírez, 80
Drake, Sir Francis, 3–4
Drury Lane Theatre, 34, 36
Du Bruit, Maître, 126–128

Ebensee prison, 112
Edison, Thomas, 136
Electron Utilization, 74
Elizabeth I, 29
Elizalde, Manuel, Jr., 6–21
Enricht, Louis, 2–3
Etheric Force, 132, 135–136, 139

Ford, Henry, 2–3
Fougeron, Loïck, 71, 78
Franklin, Charles, 136

German Security Service, 92, 94–95, 104, 109
Globe Theatre, 26
Golden Globe Yacht Race, 70, 84
Greatest Show on Earth, 68
Grover's Mill, New Jersey, 40, 43–44

Hallworth, Rodney, 77, 79, 81, 84
Hansch, Lieutenant, 112–113
Hartzell, Oscar, 3–4
Hathaway, Anne, 29
Henry II, 33, 39
Herring, Senator Clyde, 53
Hitler, Adolf, 94
Howell, Bill, 71, 78
Humbert, Frederic, 119–120, 122
Humbert, Gustave, 120, 123

Ireland, Samuel, 22–25, 26–31, 33, 36–39
Ireland, William Henry, 22–30, 32–39
Iten, Oswald, 18, 20

Jumbo, 46–69

Keely, John Worrell, 132–149
Keely Motor Company, 137, 141–143, 146–148
Kepler, Johannes, 132
King, Bill Leslie, 71, 78
Knox-Johnston, Robin, 71, 78, 79, 81, 84
Koch, Howard, 46, 47
Krueger, Bernhard, 96–102, 104–109, 111–113

Lansing, Captain, 43–44
Leidy, John, 142
Lozano, Joey, 18

Madison Square Garden, 67
Marcos, Ferdinand, 6, 10, 16, 20
Martians, 40, 48–50, 53
Mauthausen concentration camp, 111

Mindanao Island, 6
Moitessier, Bernard, 71, 78, 79
"Mr. H.," 26, 29, 32, 36–37

Nance, John, 15
Newman, "Elephant Bill," 57, 59–60, 65, 67
Nigerian Letter, 4

Operation Bernhard, 90–113

Phillips, Carl, 40–41, 43
Prince of Wales, 31

Regent's Park Zoo, 56, 59, 64
Rente Viagère, 124
Ridgway, John, 71, 78

Sachsenhausen prison, 98, 108
Sargasso Sea, 84, 85, 88
Schwend, Friedrich, 104–109
Sergeant, Henry, 136
Shakespeare, William, 22, 24–30, 32
Sheridan, Richard, 34

Tasaday, 6–21
Tasaday Preservation Fund, 10, 20
Teignmouth Electron, 71, 73, 76–80, 83–87, 89
Tetley, Nigel, 71, 78–83, 88
Toplitzsee, 113
Traun Lake, 90, 92

Vibratory Sympathy, 139–140
Vortigern and Rowena, 33–35, 39

War of the Worlds, The (novel), 46, 54
Welles, Orson, 46, 47, 51–53, 55
Wells, H. G., 46
Wilcox, James, 142

Zola, Emile, 126–128

ABOUT THE AUTHOR & ILLUSTRATOR

Photo by Laura Sawchuck

Andreas Schroeder's family emigrated from Prussia (today part of Poland) when he was five years old. As a child, he loved to read. Today, he is the author of more than 20 books of poetry, fiction, and nonfiction and has earned award recognition for his first novel, his nonfiction writing, and for his investigative journalism.

Andreas has written several books for children and adults on the subject of hoaxes. For 12 years, he also reported on swindles and deceptions from around the world for a popular national radio program.

Rémy Simard is a cartoonist, commercial artist, and award-winning author and illustrator. His work has appeared in a wide variety of books, magazines, and newspapers. He lives in Montreal, Quebec.